Your Calling
as a Leader

SEE ALSO

Jocelyn
Wheaton

Your Calling as a Leader

Gary Straub
Judy G. Turner

CHALICE
P R E S S
ST. LOUIS, MISSOURI

Cover and interior design: Elizabeth Wright

Visit Chalice Press on the World Wide Web at
www.chalicepress.com

10 9 8 7 6 5 4 3 2 1   05 06 07 08 09

Library of Congress Cataloging–in–Publication Data

Straub, Gary.
  Your calling as a leader / Gary Straub and Judy G. Turner.
    p. cm.
 ISBN 10: 0-827244-12-6 (pbk. : alk. paper)
 ISBN 13: 978-0-827244-12-6
 1. Christian leadership–Christian Churches (Disciples of Christ)
I. Turner, Judy G. II. Title.
 BX7326.S76 2005
 262'.14663–dc22

                                                    2005013224

Printed in the United States of America

Contents

Preface

It's not working...It is *sooooooo* not working!

Leaders of congregations look around on Sunday morning and wonder, "Where is the next generation of leaders?" As the current leaders grow older and more tired, this question seems more and more urgent.

Congregations across the U.S. and Canada look for ministers. Search committees look at the small stack of profiles supplied by the regional minister and say, "But where are the ministers with the qualities and experience we need?" Disciples' seminaries, though overwhelmingly under-funded, seek to do their part in turning out succeeding generations of ministerial leadership. Some statistics seem to indicate only about 50 percent of seminary graduates enter the parish or congregation, and 30 percent of them wash out. Additionally, the majority of students begin theological work much later in life than the previous generation of ministers did, which considerably shortens their span of service.

The shrinking leadership pool affects every manifestation of our lives as Disciples. Mature and experienced congregational pastors voice enormous reluctance to step into leadership in the realm of regional/general ministry. All the progressions that used to be a given—like moving on from parish life to "bigger and better things"—may no longer be assumed. Believe us when we say: "That's a good thing!" Many of our most effective and competent ministers recognize that life "down in the trenches" of parish life is where the action is, so they deliberately choose to remain engaged in this ministry. This shrinks the wider leadership pool even further and causes search teams to agonize either because they know the candidate's foibles all too well or they have no clue who the person really is before God.

As good minds across the church address this leadership crisis, signs of hope begin to appear. For example, the Division of Higher Education recently reorganized itself. It has nimbly done so, focusing on leadership development. Now known as Higher Education and Leadership Ministries (HELM), its leaders keyed off an idea currently out of vogue in many circles, namely, identifying potential leadership through Chi-Rho, CYF, and Camp and Conference networks, as well as coaching our college youth.

Several of our Disciples seminaries offer "Explore Your Call" weekends. Pastors identify high school youth who may have the gifts and call for professional ministry and bring these young people to the weekend event. During the weekend, the high school students hear effective ministers and the brightest and best divinity students talk about their call and their lives in ministry. The dialogue at these events involves honest questions and honest answers about the challenges professional ministers face. Still, the energy generated by ministers who love their vocation and divinity students who are excited about their seminary journey builds through the weekend. The trend has shifted (back) toward identifying and inviting our high school youth to consider a call to ministry early on. Mentoring them through the difficult spiritual passages of youthful years is not a novel idea. It's as old as Samuel and the elderly priest Eli. And it works.

Signs of hope are appearing in the local congregations. Some ministers and lay leaders intentionally develop relationships with young people in whom they see leadership potential to help the young people grow in Christian faith and service. Some take young people along as they make visits so that they can learn how to offer care. Innovative ministers help lay leaders of all ages grow spiritually and grow in their leadership skills.

The T-12 process shared in this book is one design for a minister working with a small group of lay leaders over a period of time. Lay leaders in many congregations are taking the initiative to learn about vital, growing congregations. As part of planning for the future of their congregation, one group of lay leaders visited vital, growing congregations in their area. After worshiping with each congregation, they discussed with one another what they saw as effective in that congregation, and also discussed what did not fit with the beliefs and values of their own congregation. They noted principles that they wanted to apply as they prayerfully developed the vision for the future of their congregation.

Of course, it is not enough to decry the yawning gaps in our leadership pool, cringing and wringing our hands saying: "Isn't it awful?" It is simply time for new models of church leadership to emerge. Let's not *deplore* the leadership crisis; let's *explore* a different model of leadership. Recently Patricia Brown offered what seems to be a guiding image in her phrase **"learning to lead from your spiritual center."**[1] What if we began to take seriously this possibility? This line captures the imagination, because it embraces the vital source of all leadership that is spiritual: the deep center of our being where we live with God. As our imaginations explore what leading out of our spiritual center might actually look like in real time, some possibilities glimmer:

1. **Our leaders have "got a life,"** that is, a vital devotional life that sustains their own soul and illuminates their leadership vision and hope. Whatever the particular practices that sustain this personal life with God, nothing can substitute for *having* a "real life" with God, a life faithfully tended and attended.

2. **Our leaders will choose to lead with their strength out of the deep center of their souls,** centered in Scripture and the life of prayer. While many methods and techniques may be engaged, in the Protestant expression of Christianity, Word and prayer are primary.

3. **Our leaders are themselves willing to be led;** that is, allowing for the leading of the Holy Spirit. This requires an inner life devoted to listening, a life that is inwardly ordered

---

[1]Patricia Brown, *Learning to Lead from Your Spiritual Center* (Nashville: Abingdon Press, 1996).

by obedience to God and surrendered to the Spirit inasmuch as it is humanly possible to do so.

4. **Our leaders lead by inspiration,** not manage by objective. Our times call for bold, prophetic leadership not only in matters of social justice and world peace, but in visioning and direction-setting guidance for our congregations, our regions, and our denomination.

5. **Our leaders are willing to ask the hard question:** How does this relate to the heartbeat of our mission: the great commission?

In this book we will work with these "glimmers," fleshing them out with examples of how real people in real congregations are learning to lead out of their spiritual center. It will quickly become clear that this book is not about some quick-fix program led by a celebrity consultant for our denominational leadership. We are not suggesting a new seminary course. We are calling on the church's leaders to rise up and fully become Spirit leaders, letting the Spirit change the whole course of our lives as we live before God.

This little book was born out of two conversations. First, Gary Straub had an afternoon conversation with Trent Butler, editorial director at Christian Board of Publication. He had just returned from a luncheon in Nashville honoring a Kenyan pastor whose spiritual vision and leadership has joined Americans, Kenyans, Sudanese, Tanzanians, Ethiopians, Ugandans, and others in a sweeping evangelistic thrust to win East Africa to Christ and to renew the church. Trent has participated in several volunteer mission trips in which he has served under this remarkable African leader.

This extraordinary Kenyan minister has led literally thousands of young Africans toward a saving relationship with Christ and has been a quiet, inspirational figure in many congregations of that continent. Hearing a bit of this story, Gary told Trent: "this man is what I call a 'Spirit Leader.'" As they were lamenting the vacuum in spiritual leadership, Trent challenged Gary to pray about whether this very conversation might be a divine nudge toward writing a small collection of reflections on spiritual leadership.

Prayerful reflection led to a second conversation, this time between Gary and Judy Turner, whose strong ministry in the parish and years of practical, effective consultation with congregations on growth and vitality made her contribution to this conversation invaluable. Gary caught up with Judy outside Eureka Springs, Arkansas, where she and her husband John are pioneering a spiritual leader training ministry called "Christview Ministries." They provide mentoring at the Christview Ministries Center in a beautiful rural setting. Judy and John often go out to other locations to lead workshops and offer leader development resources through a Web site (www.christviewmin.org).

This talk almost immediately settled into a deep place of spiritual agreement about the need for "Spirit Leaders" to emerge in these days.

The results are for the reader to discern.

GARY STRAUB, JUDY G. TURNER,
First Christian Church, Christview Ministries,
Frankfort, Ky. Eureka Springs, Ark.

Transformation Sunday,
February 6, 2005

P.S.: Because our ministries have involved a lifetime of consultation work on spiritual vitality with a wide variety of regions/congregations in all kinds of settings, and we have both had the privilege of providing the "care of souls" for so many individual believers across these years, we have made a very deliberate effort in our stories and examples to help maintain anonymity. We acknowledge a profound debt of gratitude to the people of God, for they have served as our "rabbi" on occasions too numerous (and too embarrassing) to even begin to mention. We simply join them to sing: "Praise God from whom all blessings flow!"

What Is a "Spirit Leader"?

"Spirit Leaders" are ordinary people answering an extraordinary call upon their lives. This is a call above and beyond the duties so typical to daily life and to congregational life. Being this kind of leader has almost nothing to do with our "official" church offices, such as deacon, board chair, elder, church school teacher, or minister. This call is infinitely deeper than whatever our "churchly responsibilities" might be. It a calling beyond even the power infused by installation or ordination in our faith community.

The call to spiritual leadership is based on the double claim of the Divine upon the soul. The first claim might be named the "claim of creation." The Genesis narrative paints a picture of God sprinkling a pinch of common dust into God's hand, then adding a touch of uncommon destiny, and breathing the Spirit of life into the human soul. This metaphor of "dust plus destiny" is witness to the psalmist's word that "I am fearfully and wonderfully made" (Ps. 139:14). Our very existence is intended to be a doxology—a weighty word of glory—to God's awesome provision and providence in which we are born. Out of sheer delight to be alive, and to be alive in God's life, we offer ourselves to love and serve.

1

The second call of God upon our souls is the claim of re-creation. This claim relates to the human need for reconciliation and redemption. Because we are so broken by the "business" of life, humankind needs a second infusion of the breath of God. Speaking with Nicodemus, Jesus alluded to the spiritual necessity of a second birth, being born from above, of Spirit (Jn. 3). This second wind, this enthusing (literally "breathing in God"), this invisible wind of the Spirit upon the soul, brings about re-creation—the transformation of our inner being and a radical reorientation toward our life-giving God. Once we catch our second breath, the call of God is upon us to become partners in the redemption and re-creation of the world.

These unique callings connect the soul with God-in-the-depths and open us to the leadership of the Holy Spirit. But spiritual leadership is more than just connection. We are talking about something beyond delight in being part of God's creation and serving in God's re-creation of the world. We allude to a leadership lifestyle, a way of being before God and with others that not only keeps us in constant communion, connection, and refreshment with the Divine, but also keeps us open and sensitive to the Spirit's leadership. Spiritual leadership requires regular refreshment from the Spirit and listening with a mind to obey, to act on what we hear. Daily discourse with the Spirit helps test whether our leadership vision, leadership plans, and leadership actions are truly the fruit of being a Spirit Leader, or just human ambitions wrapped in spiritual language.

Before you mentally roll your eyes and conjure up mild-mannered Disciples morphing into snake-handling charismatics, ask yourself: Can God trust me?

Can God trust me to be open (or at least open to being open) to the gifts and graces the Spirit constantly offers? The Spirit draws us into the Light. The Spirit illumines, convicts, and convinces. Through the Spirit we are baptized and blessed, discipled and directed, anointed and appointed for leadership in Christ's body and in the world he seeks to redeem.

Spirit Leaders are "regular folks" whose lives are lived in a continually open awareness that God's mercies bless them and make life livable. They are conscious of actually moving through life from one moment of mercy to the next. In gratitude for God's goodness, they offer up in a worshipful spirit everything they are and have on a moment-to-moment basis. Their lives are "their own," and yet "not their own." Their joy evokes a deep desire to live in such a way that their whole life is quite simply a "gift," and that gift is "offered up" to God. Paul names this in Romans 12 as joyful awe for the tender mercies of God, who sustains us with an unending outpouring of kindness upon our lives, whereby all the gifts and graces we need are provided.

However, these gifts and graces are often supplied in a manner not unlike what the folks at the Georgetown , Kentucky, Toyota Plant refer to as "just-in-time" manufacturing. This ingenious method allows the warehouse to replenish the parts bins out of which workers build cars on the assembly line *only* as the very last part currently in the bin is being used. For Toyota, this saves millions of dollars in warehouse storage and extra handling. Spirit Leaders live out of this knowledge of God's abundance, trusting that God's grace will appear in God's just-in-time way and will reverberate to God's purpose and glory. No wonder Spirit Leaders sing "all I have needed thy hand hath provided—Great is thy faithfulness, Lord, unto me!"[1]

Spirit Leaders are ordinary people who accomplish extra-ordinary things for God's kingdom and for Christ's church. They are not content to sit in prayer circles, light candles, collect neat mystical experiences, and notch their belts with nifty retreat techniques. They exude no airs of spiritual superiority. They live simply in the Spirit—not so they can feel good, but so they can learn how to serve God's purpose for their lives. They integrate

---

[1]Words by Thomas O. Chisholm, "Great Is Thy Faithfulness," © 1923, renewed 1951, Hope Publishing Co.

their Spirit encounters into human community and everyday relationships of love and loyalty. This good humor and sense of unselfconscious grace and wholeness is often a special mark of the Spirit.

Sue lives a simple life of service to God through the Disciple congregation into which she was born eight decades ago. After a WW II career as a U.S. Army M.A.S.H. unit nurse following General Patton's lightning march across Europe, she settled down and raised a family. No one around Sue ever doubts what this former Army nurse really thinks or why. Widowed many years ago, her life is devoted to practical prayer and serving the needs of others through her beloved CWF kitchen crew. The church kitchen serves as a base of operations for her Spirit Leader ministry. Friends might tease her about being Brother Lawrence's "sister," but whenever a need—of any kind—arises in the life of a family or individual, Sue's spiritual antennae are finely tuned to pick up on subtle vibrations. Her "wise woman" intuitions and her heart for God move heaven and earth to meet that need. All this without any fanfare that calls attention to herself in any way, yet she clearly leads with her spirit.

Mary Ann has just been elected elder chair at her church in a posh suburb. The aging facility is still stunning, but the underbelly of the congregation has been riddled with scandals and gossip while the elders conduct monthly sessions that resemble mini board meetings, focusing on property issues and ignoring the spiritual disarray. Enthused by the spiritual vision of her new pastor, Mary Ann took it upon herself to literally rearrange the furniture of the elders' meeting. No more rows of chairs facing a lectern and microphone! She centered a circle of chairs around a worship table, lit a candle, and focused the conversation on key spiritual practices, such as meditation on scripture, as ways into God's presence and toward consensus-building through discernment. These practices are beginning to feed the elders' souls.

She has taken some heavy hits from the executive and admin-istrative types for her firm rule: *no* business in elders' meetings!

She has even been known to "blow the whistle and call a foul" when someone starts talking business. Her courageous insistence makes the walk Daniel took through the lion's den look like a frolic in the park! However, after six months, the elders have started teasing her about her leadership style, which among Disciples means they like you!

Although only in his early fifties, Ralph could retire tomorrow if he wanted to, so you know it's not about the money. At 5:00 every morning, as he begins his hour-long commute to work, his car becomes his cathedral. He prays, sings, and meditates as much as driving 80 miles per hour will allow! He told his minister, Chuck, that, by the time he arrives at his desk, "I pretty well have my marching orders for the day." When someone in the community is dying, Ralph feels called to that person's side, almost compelled to befriend and companion him or her through the toughest passages at life's end. Ralph has the spiritual gift of getting next to people, and he is not afraid to talk about *any*thing. He has walked many a dying soul—friends and strangers—down through the dark valley of the shadow. Because these losses break his heart, he wonders aloud to Chuck: "How do I get myself in the middle of these mine fields?"

His minister tells him: "Because God can count on you to follow orders!" Here is a tough-minded and high-powered executive who is a highly unlikely Spirit Leader. Ralph never quite seems to understand that his faithfulness in following God's nudges is exactly what brings the next nudge his way!

Each of these Spirit Leaders is captivated by the joyful abundance that makes it possible for them, at least in their better moments, to live as Jesus lived—in communion and worshipful connection with God. They rest in what might simply be called "the blessed assurance." Who they are before God is the central core of who they are before others. This kind of authenticity and integrity allows certain things in the soul to be "deeply settled." It is clear that these people's lives are no longer "all about them." People who lead out of this abundance and assurance are mighty forces and resources in the spiritual realm.

This brings us to a word about spiritual giftedness. We have yet to meet an ordinary person doing extraordinary things for God who does not possess a deep sense of giftedness. Spirit Leaders are not prima donnas who take on some sort of "spiritual celebrity" status. However, when a person discovers what Frederick Buechner calls the intersection "where your deep gladness and the world's deep hunger meet,"[2] all the gifts and graces needed to offer that particular service are quietly supplied. This surrender to delight in obeying God serves to release an astonishing energy that echoes Paul's famous Philippian affirmation: "I can do all things through [Christ] who strengthens me!" (4:13). In fact, many Spirit Leaders report they experience graces and gifts they didn't even know they had until they stepped up to meet a fresh challenge or a tough assignment.

Isn't it time we Disciples gave up our paranoia about the self-aggrandizing abuse of spiritual gifts and simply relax, recognize, and more fully rejoice in the blessings of spiritual gifts?

The search, discovery, and exploration of the positive use of our spiritual gifts are intended to be a grace in our lives, so that we need not stress and strain, trying to do God's work without God's strength. Gifts can be both job descriptions for our next ministry assignment and joys that carry us to new depths in our desire for union with God. Quite often the healing and integration of our own inner wounds bring gifts that make new ministry possible. Spirit Leaders know this joy.

What, then, are Spirit Leaders? Spirit Leaders really are ordinary people who become aware of God's call, choose to live in radical openness to God, and exercise their gifts where God's Spirit nudges them into service.

Questions for Reflection

1. What helps you keep in close communication with the Holy Spirit?

---

[2]Frederick Buechner, *Wishful Thinking: A Theological ABC* (New York: Harper & Row, 1973), 95.

2. To what degree can God trust you? What does this trust look like in real life? In what areas could you become more trustworthy?

3. Does "gratitude for God's goodness" describe your attitude through most days? How are you living out the generosity of Jesus?

4. Have you experienced God's "just-in-time" provision? What did you learn through those experiences?

5. How have you come to understand the place of "feeling good" in the life of a Spirit Leader–a primary motivation, a desired outcome of obedience, a gift of grace?

6. Name an occasion or example from your life of integrating divine encounters into everyday relationships.

7. If a description of "integrity" is a 100 percent correspondence between who you are before God and who you are before others, what is your percentage?

8. Have you been at "the intersection between the world's deep need and your own deep joy?" What are you learning there about your own giftedness?

Why Spirit Leaders Matter

If, as we said in chapter 1, Spirit Leaders really are ordinary people who become aware of God's call, choose to live in radical openness to God, and exercise their gifts where God's Spirit nudges them into service, no wonder we need their leadership in the church now more than ever before!

We need them because all our secular models of leadership have run their course, leaving us bankrupt and bereft. We thought the latest Harvard management technique could preserve the church—exactly as we want it to be—ad infinitum. We thought if we could just reorganize ourselves around the schemes mapped out in the latest business books, we would be saved. If we could just restructure ourselves (again), we could probably last another decade or two. Alas, like those despairing disciples shambling along Emmaus Road, we can only stumblingly repeat "but we had hoped…" (Lk. 24:21a).

Spirit Leaders are *so* done with this kind of conversation that they refuse to even listen to such pitiful rehearsals of our reversals. They get up and walk out on hand-wringing gripe sessions that bemoan the sad state of our denominational affairs. Nothing gained here! The trail of dust shaken off their feet is a witness to how done Spirit Leaders are with organizational fixes.

And yet when we are honest with ourselves, the organization desperately needs fixing. It seems counterintuitive that such "fixing" can only come through an infusion of the Spirit, and this connection to the Spirit comes through the souls of Spirit Leaders. This seems to be where we are. The church and our attendant institutions face a life-or-death dilemma. We need radical surgery, surgery that only the Spirit can perform through Spirit Leaders, yet would-be Spirit Leaders are opting out of the process. What can the church do? From whence will the Spirit Leaders we need arise? How can we encourage them to invest?

We can't help but believe God is already at work in the midst of what some experts have called the "mainline malaise" and quietly raising up a new generation of Spirit Leaders.

Why do Spirit Leaders matter?

1. Because new times demand a church led by Spirit Leaders.

We are poised on the brink of a breakthrough into new ways of being church. We are living in one of the hinge moments of history, a time not at all unlike Pentecost, the Protestant Reformation, and the Cane Ridge Revival, when God is sweeping the church clean and a new organism, a renewed body of Christ, is emerging. This new shape of the New Testament church will not come out of the brilliant scheming of some megachurch pastor. Nor will it come from some savvy business executive slapping the latest solutions from Yale School of Business on the church. This new emergence can only come of God's Spirit—God's Spirit working through Spirit Leaders, who are being raised up to bold, prophetic, and inspirational leadership.

2. Because a spiritually bankrupt church system cannot expect to find needed resources in accounts long empty.

The old prayer book confession is apt: "there is no health in us." We have tried everything humanly conceivable to prop up dying institutional structures within our denomination. Repeating past failures is the very definition of insanity for all of us. Can we own up to the truth that all human accounts are tapped out? God's church is painfully yet utterly dependent on the resources of the Spirit. Spirit Leaders draw daily from the Spirit the resources and visions necessary to transform and prepare themselves to minister to a world overwhelmed with agonizing needs at every level. We look to the Spirit for insightful energy to intervene at critical transformational points in our congregational and institutional life cycles. Until we confess our spiritual inadequacy (now there's an inadequate word!) and declare our spiritual bankruptcy, we will limp along singing Annie's "'Tomorrow" song, making nice, playing "tea party," and pretending everything will somehow be okay.

3. Because the world's problems must first be addressed in the spirit realm before we can tackle the logistics.

We need Spirit Leaders who know how to pray God on behalf of God that God's will be done on earth as God's will is always done in heaven. The crying need of the church continues to be spiritual and not material, God-centered and not human-centered, relational and not organizational. Spiritual solutions come only through the wisdom of the Spirit. God-centered living brings Spirit empowerment. This is accomplished not by means of some formulaic technique, but by choosing to live a God-centered, surrendered, Spirit-directed life. Relational renewal comes only from daily relationship with the Spirit. Spirit Leaders have such Spirit-given wisdom, empowerment, and discernment. Whatever witness and influence a church may exert will first be gained in the spirit realm. Spirit leaders elect to live in such a way as to remain so radically open to God's unfolding purposes that God begins to trust them with answers to prayer.

Here's one witness to the way Spirit Leaders emerge in the life of a real live congregation:

Old First Church has been in business for over 137 years and is justifiably proud of its rich history and tradition. But the 1950s style of doing church, which had been so marvelously effective in its golden era, was wearing a bit thin in the late 1990s.

In their better moments, the lay leaders of First Church knew transformational strategies were critical to revive them in their life cycle. Given the rapidly changing religious climate in the late '90s, it was simply too much to expect the "grand old style" of being church to last forever.

Finally the impact hit. Finding enough warm bodies and willing souls to fill all the supervisory slots needed in this top-heavy, hierarchical organization was a daunting task, but doable...until that fateful year: In 1995, the nominating committee threw up their hands and declared twenty-three vacancies on First Church's administrative board of 100+ members. Widespread dis-ease and panic filled the ranks. The hue and cry "we've never done it this way before," echoed down the hallowed hallways.

Amid this painful season of unrest, small gatherings popped up all over the church—not to fire the minister or dismiss the board chair—but to pray for this health crisis. Older members who had "seen it all" over the years testified that God was definitely "doing a new thing" in their midst. Their advice was to hold steady the course: "If we are faithful, it will be OK." The elders realized it was time for them to step up to a new level of leadership, and they began to truly focus on leading. This inspired the deacons to reinvest in serving. The result was a churchwide call for a prayer and vision retreat. A specially called board meeting convened amidst impassioned speeches and enormous anxiety that Old First Church would cease being "good old First Church." Newly emerging Spirit Leaders, timidly at first, but then ever more boldly, began to witness that God still had a mission and a future calling for their dear old church.

As they interrupted the board meeting to pray, Spirit Leaders emerged out of the silence to testify that they truly longed to belong to God's preferred future. They voted to suspend their by-laws and constitution. Trusting the Spirit, they began to live their way into a future God had in mind, as they claimed Jeremiah 29:11. They realized that very little was being written about churches in their situation. Thus they would very likely have to make their way by walking in *the* Way, step by step, making up much of their strategy as they walked along leaning into the future together. Just knowing that there was no written way and that they would have to trust God to make a way made sense to these leaders as they trusted the Spirit to lead. They downsized their bulky 100+ member board to a board of fourteen, and shifted from the antiquated (dys)functional committee system to gift-based ministries, arising out of felt, named needs and spiritual callings.

Everyone wore their "crash helmets" to church the next day, thinking the roof would cave in with the impact of change; but an odd sense of relief and gratitude carried the day. However, the backlash was not long in coming. Amidst this season of joyous spiritual transformation, a financial crisis threatened to upset the fragile new balance, as some members voiced feeling "on the outs" and "uninformed," while others felt overwhelmed and overworked by trying to lead this major shift. The facilities remodeling fund experienced a shortfall, as not everyone who pledged chose to honor their pledge and critical building repairs cost more than anticipated. After prayer and conversation, several of the Spirit Leaders witnessed their faith that God would not let this grand old church fall flat on its face.

The angel in this case turned out to be an attorney from another town. This lawyer sought an appointment with the senior minister, who thought he was a sales rep and kept ducking him. An excellent church secretary, who seemed to have a sixth sense for when something needs to happen, finally brought them together. The attorney revealed that a former member in Florida had taken a keen interest in the transition struggles and had left to the church an amount of money far in excess of any shortfall. Some saluted the church's dumb luck; others sang the doxology! There is something edifying about hearing the entire finance committee praising God and singing "all [we] have needed thy hand hath provided–Great is thy faithfulness!"[1]

---

[1] Words by Thomas O. Chisholm, "Great Is Thy Faithfulness," © 1923, renewed 1951, Hope Publishing Co.

Nothing confirms "faith becoming sight" like actual cash money held in escrow in the church savings account to pay down any shortfall in remodeling pledges. Talk about building up a Spirit Leader's faith! This concrete instance of gracious provision helped free the congregation to once again reach for their great commission mission and to be more boldly "out there," beyond the church's four walls, meeting needs in Jesus' name. The leaders continue to affirm in faith that God will provide all that is needed for the fulfillment of God's mission.

Building on this newfound faith that God will provide, they have recently given up their outdated stewardship and church budget system. They are creating an experimental "vision-casting" approach to their financial needs, which challenges them to grow a new generation of Christians who choose to live abundant lives, which they have come to describe as "simply living out the generosity of Jesus." This attitude of gratitude and abundance has done wonders for the worship atmosphere of the congregation as well!

Please understand, not a single, radical Pentecostal bone can be found in this congregation's whole body! The intellectual Disciple tradition is upheld as a standard and preserved in the assertion: "Alexander Campbell himself preached here, you know!" Yet prayer and discernment makes it abundantly clear to the newly emerging Spirit Leaders that God has a future full of loving service and faithful witness that this congregation has consistently chosen to step up to. Here is a congregation learning the spiritual value of full integration of head and heart. As the ancient Christian mystics affirmed: When the head sinks into the heart, there is fire!

At all the critical junctures in a congregation's life cycle, Spirit Leaders matter. They make all the difference in whether a congregation achieves its fuller kingdom potential or gets sidetracked into all those nattering and niggling matters to which congregations without strong, steady Spirit Leaders fall prey. Blessed is the congregation whose Spirit Leaders lift the vision, encourage each other to discover and serve out of their spiritual gifts, blow the whistle and call fouls, pray and then stay out of the way!

Yes, Spirit Leaders matter. They transform a church from a business to a spiritual organism. They discern God's direction for God's church. They face new concerns with the same divine power that Christ first gave his disciples. They put new faces on old traditions to let the church emerge as a Spirit community.

Questions for Reflection

1. With your congregation/ministry setting in mind, how do you respond to the statement, "Organizational fixes don't work, but the organization needs fixing"?
2. What kinds of things indicate a "spiritually bankrupt" church? Where does the term "paralysis of analysis" fit in?
3. What does it look like when a need is filled or a problem is solved by spiritual resources?
4. Have you experienced Spirit empowerment recently? What did this encounter teach you about God? about yourself?
5. Do you know of a church or a ministry that needs transformation from a strictly "business as usual" mentality to being "cracked wide open" by an infusion of Spirit energy? How might this transformation come about?
6. Can you name a person/instance when intense intellectual energy combined with a passionate intention for Christ's purposes to produce "fire"?

Snapshots of Spirit Leaders in Scripture

Spirit Leaders are God's everyday, ordinary people who, in the critical moment, yield up their human plans and purposes to the leading of God's spirit. While such spiritual sensitivity sounds high-minded and noble, it is difficult to know what this looks like when we see it demonstrated in the lives of real people. This is why we look to the resources of Scripture; so we connect our story to God's story, grounding our sense of God's direction and will in a "since-time-began" history of faithful follower-ship.

Here are a few biblical examples of what it might look like to see a Spirit Leader in action:

1. Spirit Leaders refuse to lose their joy!
"David dances before the Lord."

Without reading too much of the psychological dynamics of a dysfunctional family into 2 Samuel 6, it is no stretch of the imagination to say that David's wife Michal was a true daughter of her depressed father, Saul. As a woman who grew up in a household that was dominated by her daddy's dark moods, is it any wonder she ridiculed and tried to repress her husband's spirit of joy and dancing? The expression of sheer joy in the victory of God's power that returned the ark of the covenant to Jerusalem so delighted David that he was inspired to dance with all his might before the Lord.

Okay, maybe his "do the locomotion" dance was not all that graceful. Maybe he could have worn more clothes than a linen ephod! The point is David refused to allow even someone as dear to him as Michal to steal his joy. He spoke a clear-eyed word of limitation to her kibitzing. Here is a leader who is utterly undaunted by the carping, criticism, and second-guessing that takes so many of our good leaders down. David is not dancing for her, nor for the maidens of Jerusalem, but in sheer delight for the victory of God in their midst. Can you even imagine a better reason to dance?

Recently retired Bishop Rev. Leontine Kelly, the first female African American Methodist bishop, tells the story of her hurried visit to an urban parish where the pastor insisted that she meet his oldest member. Her ecclesiological schedule definitely did not allot the time; but, nonetheless...the good Bishop was at last ushered into the sick room of the old woman for a brief audience. It soon became clear that Kelly was the one granted an audience! Bishop Kelly's rushed schedule of speaking engagements fell away before the moments she spent in prayer with this dear old saint. At the last amen, Kelly rose from her knees to leave when a wrinkled hand fiercely gripped her arm and a gravelly voice whispered: "Child, don't let the devil steal your joy."

When Kelly first told this story at a Disciples General Assembly, many received it as a prophetic word about the "little foxes...that ruin the vineyards." Do you know this obscure biblical metaphor from Song of Solomon 2:15? The image describes the baby kit foxes frolicking in the vineyard and leaping up to snatch tender, newly ripened grapes off the lower vines, ruining the harvest. How often do we as leaders allow jaw-snapping cynicism and biting criticism spoil our joyful enthusiasm for God? How often does our delight in the Lord who is our strength get nipped in the bud by those who nibble away at the fruit of our labors?

Now more than ever before we need Spirit Leaders to dance their joys before God's people and invite others into the dance. Too often the only exercise God's people get in church is jumping to conclusions! Spirit Leaders can choose to change all this by determining to brook no criticism and carping that steals the joy of the Lord! If we need to speak a word of limitation that orders the criticism and silences the mean-spiritedness that destroys the spiritual enthusiasm of God's people, let us do so. We will always seek to do so in a spirit of gentleness, but we will not allow the enemy to spoil the fruit of God's good gifts. Bishop Kelly's dear old saint got it right: God's children desperately need to dance and delight in the energetic joy and blessing of God's good gifts!

2. Spirit Leaders hear *THE* voice amid the voices.
"Eli teaches Samuel 'voice recognition technology.'"

God's people have always sought to respond to divine "voice recognition." Be it the voice of tradition or the fearful voice of WNDITWB (We've Never Done It That Way Before), or the trusted voice of a gracious leader, or the panicky voice of past failures, or the screeching voice of a self-acknowledged authority turned slightly edgy, or the know-it-all voice of an overly ambitious minister, or the controlling voice of one haughty group who consider themselves the final word, every congregation hears voices it recognizes and obeys. The key is to recognize the identity of the One speaking.

During the last days of the prophet Eli, his corrupt sons, who passed themselves off as spiritual leaders, wreaked havoc by exerting their voices, drowning out their feeble father's voice of wisdom and reason, and taking God's people into a downward spiral of sad and sick disobedience. God's people were sucked into this swirling vortex because the negative voices of corrupt leaders connected to their own base instincts and self-destructive behavior, carrying them into some mighty dark places.

Amidst the chaos and moral confusion, God raised up a new generation, mentored by Eli, who learned to distinguish God's voice among the myriad of competing voices. A very unlikely young person learned "voice recognition" long before the technology was ever invented. The boy Samuel spent time in God's house and quieted his soul enough to hear God calling in the night. Spirit Leaders are people trained to listen and distinguish the Word amidst the words of culture.

Spending time in God's house and learning to listen to God's voice beneath and within the voice of other godly souls is a spiritual art that can be learned through patience and practice. First Samuel 3 offers a beautiful description of the practice of spiritual direction. Remember, it took young Samuel a number of tries before he was able to begin distinguishing the Voice among the voices.

A young dad was somewhat distractedly listening to his very "grown-up" seven-year-old daughter insistently tell him why she should be allowed to be in the Pastor's Class this year and how she was young, yes, but she was more than ready to be baptized this Easter. She continued to argue her exemption to the rule quite convincingly. After a few moments, dad cut off the conversation with this line: "*You* might well be ready, but suppose we allowed all the seven year olds at church to be baptized when pastor thinks age seven is just plain too young to understand what baptism means. Then where would we be?"

Clearly defeated by adult logic, the seven-year-old withdrew to her playroom while dad retreated to his newspaper. A few minutes later, she nosed her way under the newspaper, crawled up in her father's lap and solemnly declared: "Daddy, you just don't understand...I hear Jesus calling my name!"

Somehow, this child heard something in the depths of her soul and was being true to witness to the call. Who would withhold baptism from a child who heard Jesus calling her name?

3. Spirit Leaders learn to accept God's provision and rest.
"Elijah learns to ignore human limits."

Flush from a mighty victory over Baal's prophets at the contest on Mount Carmel, Elijah frantically flees Jezebel's wrath, only to snatch defeat from the jaws of victory (1 Kings 19).

The angel of the Lord offers Elijah room service, directing him to rise and eat the bread and drink water set before him "otherwise the journey be too much for you." Here is a powerful hint about what Spirit Leaders require to keep them emotionally healthy—feasting on the resources provided by God's hand. In days of wilderness temptation, Jesus ate—was literally "deaconed" by—the bread of angels. Hidden in the hollow of God's own hand, in a god-forsaken place, the holy bread and cup of cold water began to heal, restoring wholeness and well being to this Spirit Leader's soul. When Spirit Leaders dare to rise and eat, dare to taste and see that the Lord is good, a 'new calling' is just around the corner!

That journey lasted forty days and nights, leading finally to Horeb, the holy mountain of revelation. Bereft of emotional reserves, drowning in waves of exhaustion, Elijah is pushing the outer limits of his energy and endurance just to crawl into the cave and collapse. We witness the great prophet reduced to a gelatinous glob of quivering protoplasm. Not a pretty sight! When the gauge on our spiritual reserve tank reads "E" for empty, we assume it means "enough" and coax ourselves along on mere fumes. We risk serious emotional damage, if not spiritual break-down. So, the only person surprised when self-pity seizes Elijah's soul and takes him down into the pit is Elijah. In this sad state of the soul, all his marvelous intuitive, spiritual strengths are turned against him, and he actually begins to believe the devil's lie that God has abandoned him. Self-pity opens us to enormous self-deception, doesn't it?

But the moment of our importunity is often God's opportunity. The still, small voice ministers mercy even while posing the question: "What are you doing here?" What is he doing indeed! What Elijah desperately needs and longs for but cannot name in his muted and defeated condition is the healing of the purpose of his life. This healing of purpose happens only when we are pushed up against the reason for our existence. Only when God begins to ask the core questions of our lives can we hope to recover any sense of the Divine calling upon our lives.

4. Spirit Leaders learn that words get in the way of deeper prayers.
"Samuel's mother Hannah prays God's promise into reality."

Here is a woman who, out of the depths of her barrenness and her own unspeakable suffering, began to pray. So deep was the heart-cry of her soul that her prayer was literally beyond words. Apparently even the old priest Eli had never quite encountered the likes of Hannah's fierce determination to receive the Lord's mercy and deliverance, because 1 Samuel 1:13 tells us he mistook her wordless prayer for drunkenness. Yet Hannah's silent prayer of intercession prevailed, as she somehow moved the heart of God. God honored her faithfulness, as she became the mother of the prophet Samuel. Her profound openness to God and utter boldness in prayer brought a strong season of triumph to Israel's life, in ways far beyond Hannah's imagination and hopes. She conceived and eventually gave birth to a Spirit Leader to take away the shame and humiliation of God's people.

There is little doubt that Samuel's early training in listening for God's voice with a mind to obey arose from his prenatal patterning after the heart of a soul so faithful to God and yet so strongly insistent on asking for the grace she needed. God's people in every age are humbly dependent on the power of "Hannah" prayers. Spirit Leaders are terribly hindered in their leadership of God's people unless they have the power of this profound "prayer beyond words" undergirding them.

5. Spirit Leaders embody God's energy.
"Barnabas offers the power of encouragement."

Every Sunday school child remembers something about the missionary journeys of Paul and Barnabas, but seldom do we recollect the quiet power of Barnabas' calling. His name literally means "son of encouragement" (Acts 4:36–37; 11:23–24) He was the soul whose gentle hospitality opened doors. He had a "Holy Spirit" role to play in Paul's apostolic calling. When no believer trusted the sincerity of Paul's conversion, Barnabas came alongside Paul in true "Paraclete" fashion to sustain and support Paul's calling to a teaching and preaching ministry. Spirit Leaders have this Barnabas-like power to evoke and encourage the callings of others.

Whenever they were persecuted, Barnabas dusted Paul off, raised him up out of the rock pile (Acts 14:19–20), and pressed on to their next assignment. No doubt Paul had Barnabas' courage in mind when he wrote to the Corinthians that though he was knocked down many times, he was never knocked out! No wonder Paul did not lose heart! He had the very spirit of encouragement at his side! (2 Cor. 4:7–10, 16). Spirit Leaders possess a persistence that goes way past mere human stubbornness because they see beyond the rocks, to *the* Rock!

Barnabas must have displayed a genuinely humble and graceful attitude when he disagreed with the prickly little apostle over Paul's flat refusal to share the work with John Mark. Even though the famous duo went their separate ways, Paul was later able to swallow his pride enough to admit that he needed Mark and that he proved useful in ministry (2 Tim. 4:9–11). Paul doesn't come right out and say, "Sorry, Barney, you were right," but the good humor with which Barnabas was able to flex kept alive the spirit of reconciliation.

Spirit Leaders don't need to have a heavy-duty ego stake ("See, I told you I was right!") in the outcome of personality clashes. They don't even need to hear an apology because they choose to live on the Easter side of the cross, where the selfish self is dead, buried, and out of the way, so the deeper self that is aligned with Christ may rise to faithfully serve.

It may well be that the early church survived many a leadership crisis eased by "Doctor" Barnabas' Balm of Gilead! Distrust and personal disagreement were not the last word because this Spirit Leader understood his calling of "coming alongside to help."

An inexperienced but energetic rookie minister was called to serve as senior minister of a prestigious old downtown congregation desperately clinging to the hope that tomorrow when they woke up it would be 1953 again! Jack was a much beloved senior elder in this congregation. He retired from a little five and dime store he ran for decades and knew the life story of nearly everyone in the church.

Rather than burden the young minister with his pastoral knowledge, he would simply knock gently on the pastor's door nearly every day and say: "Got anything you need done today?" After a few months of giving Jack the brush-off, the rookie reverend was finally desperate enough to be in desperate need of some quiet advice. Without getting his ego in the way, Jack offered wholehearted, well-seasoned counsel with a little twinkle in his eye that said: "You've got the hang of it now, keep up the good work!"

For the next decade, Jack played a "Holy Spirit" role in this young minister's life, guiding him through the rocks and shoals of raucous board meetings, teaching him how to deal with blustering threats from members who were no longer getting their way, helping him shore up shaky finances, and providing a heads up on potential new members moving to town. Every rookie pastor needs the "Barnabas ministry" of some saint who comes alongside to help.

6. Spirit Leaders refuse to count the cost.
"Lydia has an open heart and an open home."

At the end of their missionary journey, when Paul and Silas were remembering the times they enjoyed the most, they probably thought of the days they spent at Lydia's house in Philippi. They remembered how God opened her heart on first hearing their message that day they met her at the river. Then she opened her heart to them and insisted they come and stay at her house. Her hospitality must have provided a welcome respite from nights spent sleeping on the hard ground or aboard ship. They stayed with her until they crossed some closed-hearted people and ended up spending the night in the Philippi jail, with their feet in stocks and bleeding from a severe beating. After God miraculously delivered them, what a joy it must have been to return to Lydia's house.

Lydia was a person of means. She had a business and a large enough home to house guests. From the day of her turning to Christ, she generously offered what she had for Christ's cause. She didn't hesitate to consider what the neighbors would think when these scruffy missionaries arrived at her house. She didn't worry about whether she might need the space for other guests. She didn't calculate what it would cost to feed these men for however many days they stayed. She saw these Spirit Leaders needed a place to stay, and she offered her home.

Lydia was a brand-new Spirit Leader. She spontaneously and generously shared what she had to meet the needs of other Spirit Leaders. Her invitation to the missionaries demonstrated the generosity and wide-open hospitality of the God she had just met in Jesus Christ.

We hope the reframing of these brief stories sends a shimmer of possibility rippling across your sanctified imagination. May glimmers of specific instances arise that fit the shape of your God story!

Sensitivity to the inner realm of God, living more by faith and less by sight, and bearing witness to the indomitable spirit that is God's victory arising out the wreckage of human dreams—these are just a few of the elements to look for that help connect our story with "The Story."

Questions for Reflection

1. What kinds of things rob you of your joy in the Lord? How can you halt this robbery in progress?
2. How do you distinguish the voice of God from other voices? Who helped you learn "voice recognition"? Is there someone you can help with "voice recognition"?
3. Have there been times in your experience when you had to "ignore human limits" as you followed God's leading? How have you experienced God's provision in these times?
4. How have you been able to provide for the needs of other Spirit Leaders from the material blessings God has given you?

5. Name a time and a place when you cried out to God from the depths of your being for some great need in your life? How has God addressed your need? Is God addressing your need now? Where does this profound encounter lead?

6. What role do you think "intention" plays in encouraging others? Do people intend to encourage, or does their "embodiment of God's energy" simply flow out of who they are and give strength to those around them?

4

The Spirit Leader's Calling

What Is My Calling?

Sincere Christians struggle with this question, and with good reason! We hear others say, "I am doing what God called me to do." They seem to know exactly how God wants them to use their God-given time, energy, and abilities. But that's not the way it works for us. We have never been quite as clear about knowing what our calling is. Some Christian young people intensely seek God's direction in their lives, but go from place to place and job to job not thinking they have yet found "it." Some middle-aged Christians live in an aura of sadness thinking they have somehow missed their "calling." Some older Christians feel they have not fulfilled their purpose in life because they never managed to find *the* "thing" God wanted them to do.

Primary Calling

This way of thinking about calling, though sincere, is misdirected. This thinking focuses primarily on what we *do* for God. Spirit-led thinking centers on who we *are* in Christ. Who we are in Christ is the beginning point for finding our calling. Our **primary calling** is to grow in experiencing life as Jesus did when he lived on earth. Jesus experienced life in a trusting, loving, intimate relationship with God. This intimate relationship shaped his thoughts, emotions, character, values, and actions. Out of this relationship, he did the work of God. Out of this relationship he made an ultimate difference in the lives he touched. God calls every person who follows Christ to grow in living the intimate Spirit-led life, as Jesus did. With his Holy Spirit living within us, we can grow in loving relationship with God. This relationship will lead us to do God's work in the world. But we can *do* only because of who we *are*.

Apart from a growing love relationship with God, we cannot figure out what God wants us to do with our lives. The most important question is not, "Have I found *the* 'thing' God wants me to do with my life?" The most important question is, "Am I becoming who God calls me to be in Christ?" Some indicators help us affirm that we are fulfilling our primary calling from God. We know this when we can say: I am...

- sensing and enjoying God's presence more than I did yesterday
- trusting God more today than I did yesterday
- expressing more compassion and concern for the people around me than I did yesterday
- realizing I am more trustworthy today than I was yesterday
- caring less about what our culture values than I did yesterday
- caring more about Christ's values today than I did yesterday
- devoting more of my resources to God's work than I did yesterday

David was a church person; he had gone to church all his life. In fact, in his adult life, he went to many churches. He kept getting angry and leaving churches because the minister was not to his liking, or he did not agree with the actions of the board, or the congregation did not espouse his opinions. David had been to every church in town, and none of them met his criteria. He still thought it was important to go to church, but where could he go? One Sunday he drove out into the country and saw a little frame church with some people going in the front door. He parked the car and followed them. They were studying the New Testament book of the *Acts* of the Apostles. Something about their approach intrigued David. These people really believed the Holy Spirit is still active in the world, shaping lives, shaping the community of believers, impacting the course of human history. David kept going back to the study at that little country church. He sensed the presence of God in his life as he never had before.

At the conclusion of this study of the book of Acts, David made a point of visiting a family member, a young minister, from whom he had been alienated for years. Years ago, David had accused this minister of not being a Christian because he did not share David's political opinions. David told the young minister about going to the little country church and participating in the study of Acts. David said, "I can clearly remember the day during that study when it dawned on me God is about building bridges between people, not building walls." He paused, and continued, "I just thought a young minister would like to know what changed someone like me. It was the Word and Spirit of God."

Healing and forgiveness flowed through their conversation. Within a month after this grace-filled reconciliation, David died. The young minister conducted his funeral, celebrating that toward the end of his life, David had experienced life shaped by the Word and Spirit of God and had fulfilled his Christian calling.

Calling to Specific Works

Our primary calling is to growth in Christ-like ways, which flows from a growing love relationship with God. In daily living with a living God, we may sense an invitation to join God in **specific works** in the world. When we offer ourselves in carrying out these works, we make the love and power of God visible and tangible for other people. Our faith is also strengthened as we experience the power of God flowing through us.

Ann is a leader in her congregation, an inner-city church that has experienced gradual decline in membership in the last twenty years. The congregation was getting smaller and older. Ann felt deep grief as she thought about the church "just dying out." She prayed earnestly for the renewal of the congregation and asked if God had something yet for the congregation to do. One day while driving to the church, she noticed an elementary school within a block of her church. In all her years of church, this was the first time she had realized a school stood so close to the church.

"Then I thought about the retired teachers in our congregation," Ann says. "I'm a retired teacher myself. Then it clicked. I felt God was inviting me to gather a group of teachers and form a tutoring ministry for kids in that school." Ann talked with other retired teachers. She talked with school officials. At first, several of the teachers went into the classroom several days a week. Then, they cleaned the dust and cobwebs out of unused Sunday school classrooms at the church for an after-school ministry, which included snacks and help with homework. They asked local businesses to donate computers for a computer lab. Ann shows guests who visit the church the "state of the art" computer lab and says, "With our volunteer tutors who care about each child, this is how we make the love of God real for kids in this community."

Robert is in his 30s. The business world has long recognized his leadership skills and creative ideas, as he achieved status as a corporate executive. Seeking to follow Christ, he remains active in his congregation. One Sunday an unkempt woman showed up at church asking for money to pay the rent so she wouldn't get kicked out of her apartment. Robert noticed that the overworked pastor was the one trying to deal with this need on a Sunday morning. The woman left with a bag of groceries from the church's food pantry. "We have no way of checking out whether her need is valid," said the pastor, "but we can always give food."

"We can do better than that," thought Robert, as he felt a nudge from God. Robert prayed and came up with the idea that all the churches in the community could network to respond in Christ's name to "the least of these." With his leadership ability, he was able to get the churches to join together in identifying what people in the congregations could do to help people in need. Mechanics could repair cars. Carpenters could do home repairs. Many people could provide transportation. Others could care for children for a couple of hours.

Robert put forward the vision of a computer with a database containing information about the people resources in each congregation. This database could also provide records of who was helped and how. This would minimize fraud and help with good stewardship of the resources. Robert's vision included employing a Christian director to oversee this "Care Network" with volunteers responding to people in need with the love and compassion of Christ. Many of the churches responded to the vision, funded it, and made it a reality.

Responding to God's invitation to specific works is like throwing pebbles of love, mercy, and justice into the lake of human need. The effects can spread out in ripples, affecting more lives than we may ever be aware of impacting. The works make God's love visible and tangible, not only to the people for whom the works are intended, but also for those who observe the works. God invites us not only to do good works for the community but also to make clear why we are engaging in the works of love, mercy, and justice. In the course of doing the works, Spirit Leaders are continually and intentionally seeking ways to point people to God who is known through Jesus Christ.

At the conclusion of the tutoring sessions, Ann hugs every child and says, "Jesus loves you so much." She puts a note in the child's pocket or backpack with an invitation for the child's family to come to an event at the church.

Robert works with the director of the Care Network in training the volunteers to pray with the people they serve. When Robert gets a chance to talk about the Care Network, he says, "I do this because I have received the love and compassion of God."

Calling to Vocation

Spirit Leaders often find that God's invitation to specific works leads us to an ongoing life service for Christ. Instead of experiencing the work we are doing with God as a "spare time project," it becomes the shape our lives take. The project now forms part of our spiritual identity.

This is particularly true if the works require the use of our spiritual gifts. Spiritual gifts are those special abilities God gives us and the Holy Spirit infuses in us to use in the ongoing ministry of Christ and in strengthening his church. Discovery of spiritual gifts often leads to discovery of vocation. Vocation may involve compensation and provide means of livelihood for a leader, or vocation may be the way a leader serves Christ while making a living doing something not obviously related to Christian service.

Lillian earns her living as an accountant. Since everyone in her church knew she was good with numbers, they asked Lillian to serve as church treasurer; and she did so for years. Nobody really understood Lillian's feelings. For her, doing the church treasurer job year after year felt like serving a life sentence. Other church members did pick up on how Lillian often seemed unhappy and expressed negativity in church meetings. Lillian's life changed when her congregation offered a spiritual gifts workshop. A new, life-changing thought dawned for Lillian when she heard that God wires people differently to do different kinds of service. In the course of the workshop, she identified "encouragement," "leadership," and "intercessory prayer" as her spiritual gifts.

Since her work as church treasurer was not directly related to any of these gifts, she found the courage to resign that position. She immediately felt relief and prayed for God to lead her into new areas of service in which she could work out of her giftedness. She got involved in leading workshops to help others discover their spiritual gifts and counseled others on how they could develop and use their gifts through the ministries of the church. Largely as a result of Lillian's work, the church changed its way of operation from recruiting people to fill the institutional slots, to helping people discover their gifts and plug into ministries that need those particular gifts. Many in the congregation, like Lillian, are discovering their vocation. Although Lillian still earns her living as an accountant and seeks to be a Christian witness in her work, she says her vocation is encouraging Christians in their gifts.

Joyce taught college courses. She was a teacher and believed her lifelong vocation to be college teaching. Doing the research and preparing lectures challenged her intellect. Seeing students grasp new ideas and concepts proved exciting. She believed she was contributing to their lives. Little did Joyce know that a phone call on a Saturday evening could change the direction of her life. The pastor of her church called to say he was sick. "Can you give the sermon tomorrow?"

She said yes, and hung up the phone. Then panic struck. "What have I done?" she thought. "I'm a teacher, not a minister." She prayed, worked with a scripture passage, heard God's word to her through the passage, and wrote an outline. The next day, as she shared the message with the congregation, an inner voice said, "This is what I was born to do." Although others in the congregation affirmed her preaching and said she should preach more often, she rejected the idea. It did not seem possible to change direction, go to seminary, and become a professional minister. But when she wasn't aware of thinking about anything in particular, mental pictures came of her preaching and leading a congregation. It was as if a life devoted to ministry was already forming within her. It would not let her go. She still loved college teaching, but felt an unfulfilled longing to be a spiritual guide as well as a teacher. Still she didn't tell anyone about the inner stirrings.

A student came to Joyce's office to talk about the difficulties the student experienced with the course. The student also talked about the problems she had with relationships and her lack of purpose in life and feeling of despair about the future. Joyce thought, "These are spiritual issues. If only I were her pastor, I could offer more than I can offer as her teacher." That encounter with the student did it! Joyce made an appointment with her regional minister to explore ordination. She discovered that she could pastor a small church part-time while she went to seminary several days a week. She resigned her teaching position, taking a considerable cut in salary. Several years into this new life in professional ministry, she had a conversation with her pastor over lunch.

"You know you started all this by getting sick on a Saturday!" she said with a laugh. Then she said more seriously, "This new vocation is demanding. But every day I feel a deep satisfaction that I'm doing what I was born to do."

Marilyn makes her living as a nurse, and Gill is a building maintenance supervisor. They attended church, but what really shaped their lives for years was the dream of a lakeside home in the country. They worked hard to be able to purchase the land by the lake and devoted most of their time on weekends to building the house, doing much of the work themselves. After a number of years, they were finally able to move into their dream home. About that time Marilyn picked up a Christian magazine and read an article written by a "parish nurse." She became intrigued with the idea of a nurse who is available to visit people in their homes and is able to help with their medical needs while also helping with their spiritual needs. Though she tried to forget about it, the idea kept coming to mind. Finally, she came to terms with the fact that the parish nurse idea was not going to let go of her, so she might as well do something about it.

She realized that if she became a parish nurse, she would need to be prepared to address the spiritual needs of the people she served. This required she be more intentional about her own spiritual growth. She and Gill took part in an intensive Bible study their church offered. Gill went on a mission trip with a group from the church and used his building skills. He came back wanting to do more of this kind of serving. He got involved with Habitat for Humanity. Marilyn became her congregation's parish nurse. She visited people in their homes, sharing her medical skills and praying with them. She saw significant healing in the lives of the people she served.

One night Gill and Marilyn were sitting in their dream home. Finally, Marilyn got up the courage to say what had been on her mind. "Gill, you know we've been happier as we've grown in Christ and gotten more involved with his work. I've been thinking…if we didn't have this large house and all this yard to keep up, we'd have more time for serving." She swallowed hard and waited for him to explode and ask her if she was crazy to think about giving up their dream home.

But Gill simply said, "I've been thinking the same thing." They both cried as they placed a "For Sale" sign on their dream home. It was hard to think of giving it up or to think of living anywhere else. But they had experienced something of surpassing worth as they had responded to God's invitation to join him in specific works. As they continued using their gifts in these works, they came to identify themselves as "parish nurse" and "carpenter for Christ." In fulfilling their vocations, they experienced a joy that surpassed that of owning their dream home.

Characteristics of Calling

How can we discern whether God is calling us? You can look for several indicators.

First, the call of God is persistent. If the idea of serving Christ in a certain way keeps coming up at various times in life, if it seems to be pursuing us, not letting go, it may be the call of God. The idea of serving Christ in this way may be appealing or terrifying, usually both. If the idea is only appealing, then it should be questioned. Maybe that idea comes from our own egos and appeals to our pride or grandiosity. Wouldn't it be "neat" to do something like that and have people look up to us? Wouldn't it be "great" to do something with that kind of impact on the world and be remembered forever? Wouldn't it be "noble" to sacrifice so much and have our picture hanging in the "Christian Hall of Fame"? These are indications of the impulse coming from ego. If, however, the idea is appealing because it calls forth the best in us for Christ's cause, but it is also frightening, this may well be a mark of validity. God's plans are much bigger than our human ideas. God's work is far greater than anything that human effort can accomplish. God's calling requires that we rely on God to fulfill the call. It is frightening because it is truly so far beyond us in our unaided human abilities as to be ludicrous. In calling us, God is inviting us to join in Christ's ongoing work in the world, powered by the Holy Spirit. God is not telling us to go off and do amazing things in our own strength.

A second characteristic of call to a work of God or vocation is that other Christians confirm it. Our Christian family can sometimes see in us the gifts before we see them in ourselves. We may be taken aback in realizing that they see these gifts, but their words ring true. Other Christians can articulate a call for us when we have considered doing a work or pursuing vocation, but have been too tentative to speak it. As we hear their words, the shape of the call solidifies. A good practice in testing whether we have heard the invitation of God is to share our sense of God's call with other leaders in the church who are spiritually mature and who know us well. In a congregation whose leaders and people are open to the leading of the Holy Spirit, recognize and seek spiritual gifts, and expect Christians to venture with God, callings can be mutually discerned and encouraged.

A third characteristic of call is that it has a price. Fulfilling God's call exacts a price, demands risk and sacrifice. Moses standing before the burning bush knew the risk involved in responding to God's call to lead the people from their slavery to the land of promise. The boy Samuel saw great risk in agreeing to speak for God as a prophet. His first prophetic assignment was to tell Eli the priest (and a powerful figure) that God's judgment was coming against him. Peter willingly faced risk when he fulfilled his calling as a preacher of the gospel on the day of Pentecost. He knew his bold witness could land him in jail or even mean execution. Paul dared to endure the risk represented by both Jews and Gentiles when he responded to God's call to be an apostle. These all had to sacrifice comfort, security, reputation. Some would lay down their lives.

Yet Paul says, "I consider everything a loss compared to the surpassing greatness of knowing Christ Jesus my Lord, for whose sake I have lost all things." (Phil. 3:8, NIV) Despite the risk, despite the sacrifice, this Spirit Leader experienced a life of fullness in God that was worth so much more than anything offered through worldly power and privilege, wealth, or fame. As he risked security and joined God in his work in the world, Paul came to know God more intimately. He had personal experience of God's love and faithfulness. He found in Christ everything of true worth. He had the joy, unlike any lesser happiness, of knowing that he had a part in fulfilling God's plan and purpose for creation.

What is your calling? Moses, Samuel, Peter, and Paul, despite the risk, said yes to God's call and fulfilled God's purpose in their time. How do you fulfill God's purpose in your time? How can you know what God is calling you to be and do?

1. Focus on your primary calling to grow in relationship with God. Let the Holy Spirit guide and shape your life so that you increasingly experience life as Jesus did, loving and trusting God, and doing God's work.
2. Be alert to God's invitation to join in specific works in the world. When you see a need, do you have an idea of how you could bring the love and power of God into that situation? Do you sense that this work "has your name on it"? Do you feel a "nudge" from the Spirit to plunge in or take the next step? Take the first step in faith that you will meet God there, already at work, and God will show you what to do next.
3. If doing these works with God seems to be shaping your life in a new direction, ask God if this is a calling to a new vocation. If you have a sense that what you are already doing in serving Christ is your vocation, ask if God is leading toward a new way of fulfilling your vocation or toward a deeper commitment to it. God's call will exact a price. But saying yes to God leads to the amazing discovery of what you were born to do.

Questions for Reflection

1. What word of guidance and encouragement would you offer a Christian young person struggling to discover what God wants this person to do with his or her life?

2. How would you describe the primary calling of every Christian?

3. Think about a time in your life when you saw a need and responded to meet this need. Did this response lead to ongoing involvement with the particular need?

4. How would you describe your vocation? How is your vocation related to the way you earn your living?

5. The characteristics of God's call as described in this chapter are: (1) the calling is persistent; (2) the calling is confirmed by others; and (3) the calling requires risk and sacrifice. Which of these characteristics most resonate with your own sense of God's call? Are there other aspects of spiritual callings that you might name?

Key Spirit Leader Principles

Spirit Leaders Discern

Spirit Leaders follow Jesus and listen for his voice, which is the inner presence and guidance of the Holy Spirit.

This basic Spirit Leader principle comes from John's gospel. All other principles follow from it. As John wrote his gospel, he remembered a striking metaphor Jesus used to describe how he leads his followers–the metaphor of a shepherd and his sheep. Jesus claims, "I am the good shepherd." He paints a word picture of a sheep pen where he stands at the gate. "The gatekeeper opens the gate for him, and the sheep listen to his voice. He calls his own sheep by name and leads them out. When he has brought out all his own, he goes on ahead of them, and his sheep follow him because they know his voice" (Jn. 10:3–4). Jesus describes the life of Spirit Leaders as being followers first. Spirit Leaders follow the One who knows them, cares for them, and knows the way to their destination. Yes, Spirit Leaders follow Jesus and listen for his voice. Today we hear the voice of Jesus through the Holy Spirit.

In his commentary on the gospel of John,[1] Gary Burge shares the story told by a Westerner traveling in the Middle East in the 1980s. This traveler observed a remarkable incident in a Palestinian village near Bethlehem. In protest against Israeli occupation of their village, the citizens refused to pay their taxes. In retaliation, the officer in command confiscated all the livestock owned by the villagers. The soldiers herded hundreds of sheep into one large pen. A Palestinian widow appeared before the officer to ask for the return of her sheep. "They are my only means of livelihood," she pleaded. The officer laughed cynically and said, "Well, if you can find your sheep among all these, you can take them." A soldier opened the gate and the woman's young son pulled out a reed flute and played a simple tune again and again. A sheep stopped grazing and looked up. Then another wooly head popped up. And several more sheep raised their heads, looking attentive. Then those sheep made their way through the crowd in the pen to the gate where the boy stood playing his flute. The boy kept playing as he and his mother led their twenty-five sheep home.

How did those sheep discern the sound of the shepherd's flute from other sounds all around them? How do we learn to discern the good shepherd's voice from all the other voices we hear? Those inner nudges we feel, where are they coming from? Are they really coming from our spiritual center where the Holy Spirit is? They could be coming from influences of our culture, people around us, our own egos, evil forces in the spiritual realm, our brain chemistry. How do we learn which nudges to pay attention to and act on?

Spirit Leaders Go Deeper in Their Relationships with God

First, we continually go deeper in relationship with God. As the divine friendship expands in the center of our being, we

---

[1]Gary M. Burge, *The NIV Application Commentary* (Grand Rapids, Mich.: Zondervan, 2000), 302.

become more adept at knowing whether the inner voice we hear "sounds like" God and whether the inner nudges "feel like" God. It's like when you have a good friend, someone you know very well. You hear another person quoting your good friend. You can respond with some certainty, "That sounds just like him," or, "I don't think she would say that."

It's obvious that we get to know the people we spend time with. If we want to know God, we spend time with God. We study scripture and meditate on the meaning of the words for our lives and for the work we are doing with God. The Holy Spirit not only helps us apply the scriptures to our present situations and concerns and activities, but also helps us know God more intimately. We grow in understanding of who God is and how God works with people.

We develop a life of prayer. When we're going about our daily activities, we seek to be aware of God. We set aside times when our only agenda is to be present with God, to communicate with God, and to invite God's Spirit into the depths of our being. The Holy Spirit needs room to work, but our lives are so busy and crowded. We cooperate with the Spirit when we make space in our schedules and on our calendars.

We cooperate with the Spirit when we make inner space that is not already filled with our thoughts, plans, hurts, desires, and concerns. In making inner space we bring our "stuff" before God, willing for the divine hands to rearrange or remove any of it. We are open to the divine hands putting new things into that space. Clearing space for God is a disposition of openness and surrender. It is the disposition of Jesus, who prayed, "Not my will, but yours." As we make room for God's Spirit, the spiritual center within us will expand in response to the greatness of God. We will admire the beauty and wisdom of God to the point of wonder and awe. Our desires will change as we want more of the fullness we experience when we are in tune with God. We will experience moments on "holy ground" filled with awe. One of the greatest wonders is the realization of our own growth in loving God. As our love continues to grow, we will more frequently recognize the "voice" of God and the "nudges" that are God's touch.

As the divine friendship expands in the center of our being, we learn to distinguish the sources of the thoughts, feelings, ideas, and plans that come to conscious awareness. An awareness that comes from God often brings with it a sense of "rightness" or "peace" as we continue to ponder it and pray with it. The awareness may at first startle us, because it seems to come from "beyond" anything we could conjure up within our own minds. The awareness may frighten us because it seems to require so much from us. The awareness may humble us in owning up to the fact that we are still such beginners in the spiritual life. We may struggle with the new awareness. But if the awareness comes from the Spirit, our spirits will recognize truth and resound in accord with the Holy Spirit. We will settle into a profound peace in the center of our being. This offers a kind of confirmation—a yes-ness from the heart of God, whose word is always "yes" (2 Cor. 1:19).

If the awareness is not from God, we will likely experience a sense of dis-ease, disturbance, or unrest. Even if we try to deny truth or deceive ourselves, a sense of "not right" will linger in our souls. Instead of feeling in tune with God, we will experience dissonance. If we accept that the thought, idea, plan, or feeling is not from God and still let it live in us and produce actions in the external world, these actions may result in harm rather than good. Our love for God fades a bit, and we will no longer hunger for God's presence. However, we have a way to avoid this internal state of spiritual malaise, by owning up to our aspiration to become Spirit Leaders who follow Jesus and listen with a mind to obey the promptings of the Holy Spirit.

Some good discernment questions:

- Does this thought, feeling, idea, or plan bring with it a sense of truth and peace?
- Am I feeling unrest and disturbance? What does my inner dissonance mean?

• Is this awareness leading me toward the light of God or away from the light?

Spirit Leaders Listen to Their Own Lives

As Spirit Leaders grow in God-awareness, we also grow in self-awareness. "I've noticed that the more clearly I see God, the more clearly I see myself, with strengths and weaknesses, good intentions and not-so-good intentions, generosity and self-centeredness, hopes and doubts, faith and fears," said Tom in an elders meeting.

Linda quickly responded, "But Tom, everyone knows what a *good* person you are."

"No one in this church is more respected than you are," added Jim.

But Tom persisted. "You are all good friends, and I appreciate your kind words. But the truth is—inside, each of us is a mixed bag. In our Christian life we are on our way, but we aren't there yet. And it helps us to know what is in that mixed bag."

Tom's comment started a discussion the elders later remembered as one of their most helpful sessions. Spirit Leaders recognize their weaknesses and limits as well as their strengths. If we are not realistic about our limits of time and energy, we can teeter on the edge of burnout. If we are not in tune with our real motives, we will operate from the periphery rather than the center. On the periphery we are jerked around by people's expectations, by fears of rejection, by fear of disappointing people, by our need to be recognized as important, and by our need to be in control of groups and processes.

Kathy could always be counted on in her church to do whatever needed to be done. She served as a Sunday school teacher, was president of the Women's Group, sang in the choir, and made sure the sanctuary was in order for morning worship. One Sunday after church, the pastor approached Kathy. "Kathy, we are having a reception after worship next Sunday, and I was wondering if you could make the arrangements."

Kathy's face got tense, and she looked close to tears. "If one more person asks me to do one more thing in this church, I am going to explode!" she shouted.

The pastor guided Kathy to his study and asked her to sit down. He wrote on a pink memo pad, tore off the sheet, and handed it to Kathy. He said, "This is your pink slip. You're fired from everything you're doing for the church for three months. During that time, just come for worship and receive the love of your church family. Spend the next three months resting and praying."

Kathy protested, "But who will do all those things if I don't do them? I can't disappoint so many people."

Kathy looked down at the slip of paper. She read: "Listen to your life."

Kathy wasn't sure what those words meant, but she went home and sat on her deck for a couple of hours. She realized she had been operating on the periphery, the edge, rather than from her spiritual center. She heard the invitation to spend more time simply enjoying God's presence. She spent hours on that deck over the next couple of months. She had to confess that much of what she was doing "for God" was really "for Kathy," because she needed the approval of people. She had to confess that her spirit was so filled with the voices of "shoulds" and "oughts" and "What will people think?" that she could not hear the voice of God.

One day she felt a nudge to take some fabrics from the drawer and make something. Why not get out her grandmother's old quilt frame and make a quilt? As she cut and stitched, she felt surges of spiritual energy she had not felt in a long time. It was as if something deep within her was becoming visible as the quilt took shape, as if unseen hands were guiding her hands. The finished quilt was more beautiful than she could have imagined.

Shortly after her "spiritual sabbatical," Kathy went with a mission group from her church to a village in Mexico. She saw poverty as she had never known it. The people wanted to work, but there were no jobs. She felt the inner stirring again as an idea came. What if she taught the women in the village to make quilts? She could ask women's groups in her town to donate the fabric. She could bring back the finished quilts and sell them in the U.S. and give the village women the proceeds. She couldn't wait to get started on this spiritual entrepreneurial venture! Now, in a village in Mexico, women make quilts, and Kathy and her team sell them in the U.S. and return the money to the women. Now the women of the village are able to buy food for their children and send them to school. This all became possible because Kathy took a spiritual vacation to listen to her life. She discovered the "intersection between the world's deep need and her own deep joy."

Spirit Leaders listen to the voice of their own lives. Our confidence in God's unconditional love for us evokes in us recognition of all the sources of the different inner voices. We are not proud that voices from ego, lust, and evil intent speak from within; but it is important for us to recognize that they do. If we deny that these forces are there, we are more likely to be blindsided by them. We are more likely to say or do something that is harmful when we are not aware of the potential for harm that is within us.

An inner feeling of disturbance about something we are thinking or doing is an indication that we may be responding to some other voice than the voice of the Holy Spirit, resounding from the depths of the true self within. The true self is the person we were created by God to be and the authentic follower of Jesus we are becoming. The true self gets covered over by unhealthy and unfaithful reactions to the hurts and fears we've experienced throughout our lives. We create a "false self" with ego at the center, encrusted with layers of self-promoting and self-protecting habits.

Part of the inner journey of growing in Christ is allowing the Holy Spirit to peel back the layers, heal the underlying hurts, expose our pride, and show us how to make creative and redemptive responses to things that happen in the external world. As we cooperate with the Holy Spirit in this work of inner transformation, the ego's false-self weakens; and the true self in

Christ emerges. Living in the grace that calls us forth to be who we really are, we discover the ways of living and serving that Jesus described as the "easy yoke" and the "light burden."

Spirit Leaders Listen and Speak

When people come to the bank, they often step into Jim's office to visit with him. For some reason they feel "lighter" when they leave. Jim doesn't try to fix their problems or give them advice. He mostly gives his presence and attention; he listens. Jim says, "I try to express the love of Christ through listening to people. Being 'listened to' is so much like 'being loved,' it's hard to tell the difference!" If people ask for his advice, he usually says, "I don't know, but how about we pray together and ask the One who does?"

Occasionally Jim speaks out of the prayer of listening to say, "Have you thought about this? Have you looked at it this way?" The questions help redirect the person's own abilities and confirm Jim's words are on target. Often, a way they hadn't seen before opens up in the moment.

The church in which Jim is a Spirit Leader also benefits from Jim's gift of listening. Often in a meeting he sits quietly and attentively. At the critical moment, at just the right moment, he speaks. His words hit the bull's-eye, and everyone knows it. He offers a different perspective on the situation or proposes an idea that helps the group get unstuck or move forward in a new direction. Jim describes what he does as "two-channel listening." While seeking to be as fully attentive and present as a human can be (realizing that our minds do wander), he also seeks to be attentive to the Spirit of God. "I ask the Holy Spirit to guide me in seeing what the Spirit sees about the person or situation. But I always offer what I see with lots of humility," Jim says. "I'm never sure I'm right. I speak what I see and urge others to ask God to show them whether it's right."

Every Spirit Leader has the capacity to be a "two-channel listener." The Holy Spirit guides us in perceiving things that are helpful for the spiritual growth of others and for the well-being and growth of the congregation. Realizing our inner impressions have many sources, the wise Spirit Leader "tests" where this impression is coming from before speaking it aloud. "Does this really 'sound' like God? Could it result in harm? Am I seeking attention? Do I need to be right?"

These are helpful test questions to ask. In speaking, the Spirit Leader humbly offers what he or she thinks is from the Spirit. The leader offers it with open hands, without investment in whether it is accepted. The leader trusts that the Holy Spirit also reveals truth to others, and the leader wants to hear their perceptions. The leader believes that mutual listening and discernment is the best way to receive God's perspective and guidance. The Spirit Leader seeks to follow Jesus and invites others to join in listening for Jesus' voice through the Holy Spirit.

Spirit Leaders Courageously Act

Spirit Leaders act courageously on intuitions submitted to God. Could Moses be 100 percent sure he heard the voice of God from the burning bush? Surely the commission to stand before the most powerful ruler in the world and tell him to let his slave labor force go terrified Moses. Moses felt totally inadequate for this mission. In the conversation, God didn't give a lot of instructions or assurance of success. All Moses remembered God saying was, "I will be with you." It would have been easy to convince himself it was all a hallucination, a figment of his imagination, and go back to what he knew how to do, tending sheep. But Moses chose to act. He went with Aaron to Pharaoh and delivered God's message. In the going and the speaking, Moses received God's strength. He was on God's mission, and the strength that resides in God flowed through him. The courage to do what God called him to do emerged from within as he took steps in faith.

A similar process emerges in the lives of twenty-first–century Spirit Leaders. A clergy couple served as pastors of congregations for years. At various times, they felt nudges from God to start a training center for spiritual leaders. But how was this possible?

Their financial resources were limited. They had no confidence in their abilities as entrepreneurs or fund-raisers. Within the last couple of years the nudges came more frequently. They both had intuitions that the time for the venture was close.

"If this is really from you, God, give us some sign," they prayed. Changes in their ministry settings confirmed that it was time. But as they resigned from their pastorates, they felt like they were stepping out, off the edge of the earth, into thin air. They can't really say how they received the strength to take this step, leaving behind all tangible means of support and placing their house on the market; but that's what they did.

"They say there is a fine line between courage and fool-hardiness; but we decided that even if we fall flat on our faces, we will know we did our best to follow the best intuitions we had." From a totally unexpected source, they received a friendly loan for purchasing property for the training center. A good facility in a beautiful location became available, and they were able to buy it. Friends who believe in their God-dream support them with prayers and with donations. This is how they summarize what they have experienced in this faith venture: "Once you really get out on a limb with God, you see what only God can do. Everything we've truly needed has been provided—usually in very unexpected ways." These Spirit Leaders courageously followed Jesus, listened for his voice, and obeyed the inner promptings that came their way.

Spirit Leaders Rest

The first and second chapters of Genesis describe the creative work of the Spirit of God. The Spirit hovered over the formless void and brought forth life: light, dry land, seas, sun, stars, sea creatures, birds, animals of every description, and finally human beings. It all builds like a symphonic work, as the different created beings enter onto the stage of planet Earth and offer their praise by their very existence. When human beings make their entry, this may seem to be the highest moment of creation, the epitome of the creation story. But no, one more day rises to bring the beautiful completion and culmination. This is the climatic moment in the music. It is the pause. It is the day God rested and simply enjoyed everything that God formed and breathed into being.

Made in the image of God, we share in the divine life through Christ Jesus. God shares with us the joy of creating. We share the divine life as we engage in work, and we also share in the divine life when we cease working and focus on appreciating, enjoying, loving. God built rest into the fabric of human life by instituting the sabbath day, which God commanded God's people to honor.

Sheila pastors a mid-sized congregation, and the members appreciate the positive changes she has helped bring about in her four years of ministry there. Everyone knows Sheila works hard. Several years ago, Sheila asked for time on the board meeting agenda to discuss a personal concern. The board members felt a tinge of anxiety. What could this be about?

She began, "Friends, for the past several weeks I have felt convicted by God's spirit, because I consistently violate one of the Commandments." The roomful of people all gasped simultaneously. Now she had everyone's attention. "I have consistently violated the Fourth Commandment." Someone grabbed a Bible to find out which Commandment that was, while others were guessing which it might be and fearing the worst. "That is the Commandment to honor the sabbath day," she explained.

The roomful of people all sighed together in relief. "I'm very serious about my nonstop working being a violation of God's design for human life," Sheila insisted. "And what I propose is that I honor Mondays as my sabbath day, for rest and worship and spiritual renewal. I know my day off is Friday, but that's the day I have to clean house and run errands. In instituting Sabbath time, I think God meant for us to stop being 'productive.' I think God meant for us to do something in Sabbath time that is different from what we do to maintain life, and to focus on what gives life meaning and joy."

After working together on a system for handling pastoral emergencies, the board approved Sheila's request. Now the congregation honors Monday as "the Pastor's Sabbath," and Sheila knows she is a better minister because she honors that day for prayer, spiritual reading, and hiking. She models the importance of resting for her congregation, and they have benefited from making time for Sabbath in their weekly schedules.

Church leaders often excel at over-working, but we can't operate as real Spirit Leaders when we are over-scheduled and exhausted. It is difficult to hear God when we're always producing, always hurrying, always serving. Sabbath is about a time set apart for receiving God's goodness rather than trying to generate good things for ourselves and others, a time for being more than doing. Someone once said, "Sabbath is stopping long enough to receive blessing." Sabbath is an important reminder that we are not God. The world can continue operating without our efforts! Spirit Leaders make time for Sabbath.

Even as they are actively engaged in serving, Spirit Leaders rest in another way. They do their best, give their best, and then surrender the outcomes of their efforts. Ministry is not ultimately something we do. In the end, ministry is something we trust. We cannot by any amount of effort ensure the success of a ministry project. We cannot control what other people choose to do or how they will choose to respond. We cannot manipulate the course of things. What can we do? We can pray. We can listen for God's invitation and join in God's work. We can give generously of who we are and what we have for that work. We can be faithful. We can trust that God will use what we give for God's purpose. We can let go of our need to see particular outcomes. When we do, the sweet peace of Christ envelopes us; and we rest in him. The Spirit Leader follows Jesus and listens to his voice by taking time to rest in him.

Isn't the need to see particular outcomes often related to ego? Spirit Leaders remember that when we were baptized into Christ, ego and the false self built around ego died and was buried. We came alive in Christ. Every day is a journey toward the fullness of that life. Degree by degree we grow into Christ's life, as we choose to die to ego. To pray, "Thy Kingdom come," is also to pray, "My kingdom go." The church of Jesus Christ will not grow and thrive in our time unless it is led by disciples who are growing in Christ's life. Human ego does not discern the Spirit's depths. Human ego only builds memorials for humans. Only dead egos build live churches.

A highly successful executive retired and had time on his hands. He filled the void by coming to the church to repair and update the facility. He paid for the materials for his projects from his own pocket. His gifts of time, skill, and money could have been helpful to the congregation, but for one thing. The executive was also trying to shore up his sense of personal importance through what he gave to the church. When he completed fixing something, he made sure that people knew about it. He took offense if not enough people said "thank you." The congregation members had a shock one Sunday morning. They saw that the front doors of the church were new, and a brass plaque nailed to the doors announced that the doors were donated in honor of the executive's family!

Some leaders of the congregation went to lunch together that Sunday and talked about why they felt a plaque on the front door was inappropriate.

"The church does not belong to him and his family," said Andrea angrily. "It belongs to all of us."

"That's right!" affirmed Marge.

"Or does it?" asked Kent. "Doesn't the church belong to God? The church building should be dedicated to God's purposes and not ours. Maybe many of us have been acting as if the congregation exists to meet our needs and fulfill our desires for it. Maybe he did us a favor in nailing the plaque on the front door. It reveals in exaggerated proportions how we've *all* been thinking."

Congregations can have a corporate false self built around the egos of the people who participate in the congregation, especially the strong egos who insist on their way. The corporate false self operates according to the desires and preferences of the members. "What *I* want for *my* church" is a phrase revealing a strong individual ego with a need to control the congregation. "What *we* want for *our* church" is a phrase revealing the false corporate self.

The true self of the congregation is the nature of Jesus Christ, who came as a servant, not to fulfill his own desires, but to do the will of God. The congregation can only fulfill its true nature and purpose when disciples of Jesus surrender their personal preferences and plans so that God can fulfill God's plan for the church. Only the power of the Holy Spirit released through prayer can break through the layers of the false congregational self and free the congregation to discover their true identity as Christ's body. As disciples put aside their egos and listen together for direction from the head of the body (Jesus Christ) through his Holy Spirit, the church lives!

The key principle for Spirit Leaders is to listen for the voice of Jesus through the Holy Spirit. We grow in our ability to discern his voice from other voices as we grow in relationship with God. We discover who we really are in Christ and learn to serve most effectively as we listen to our own lives, discerning the false self from the true self in Christ. We listen for the voice of the Holy Spirit as we listen to others, and we speak out of that listening. We act courageously on impulses submitted to God. We are able to set aside times for rest and to experience renewal because we place all outcomes of our work in God's hands. God works through surrendered Spirit Leaders to help congregations discover their true identity and mission.

Questions for Reflection

1. The gospel writer John quotes Jesus as saying, "My sheep hear my voice." In your experience, what does it mean to "hear the voice" of Jesus?

2. What are some criteria you use to determine whether an awareness (thought, idea, or inner impression) is from God?

3. What spiritual practices help you grow in your relationship with God?

4. Are you trying to discern whether an awareness you are currently experiencing is from God? What might help in your discernment?

5. How do you listen for the Spirit's voice when you are engaged in conversation with another person? When you are part of a gathering or meeting?

6. When you believe you've received an insight, idea, or message that came from the Holy Spirit, how do you decide when to speak and what to say?

7. What spiritual disciplines assist you as you attempt to "listen to your life"?

8. What are some warning messages you hear when you are not living out of your true spiritual center?

9. Following the voice of Jesus through the Holy Spirit often requires courageous action. Are you holding back? What do you need in order to be able to move forward with Christ?

Spirit Leaders and Congregations

The Congregational Climate

When spring is in the air, a homeowner's thoughts turn to sprucing up the yard and buying flowers to add color. The homeowner goes to a nursery with a greenhouse, expecting to find all her old-favorite flowers and some new varieties. She walks into the greenhouse and gasps with surprise. She sees only brown, withered, and dying plants with no blooms. She notices how hot and dry the air feels and realizes the greenhouse has a serious problem with its climate control. The plants cannot thrive and blossom in that environment. She feels sadness for the plants dying in that environment and also anger toward whoever is responsible for maintaining a healthy climate in the greenhouse. But solving the problems of that business is not her mission. She goes on to another nursery with a greenhouse. Walking into the second greenhouse, she feels the refreshing cool, moist air. She sees healthy dark green plants and beautiful blossoms of many colors. She takes a deep breath, savoring the slightly sweet fragrance of health and growth.

Like a greenhouse, every congregation has factors that determine whether the environment will help or hinder the development of Spirit Leaders. If a new person from outside that congregational system walks in on Sunday morning, that guest can usually sense whether the environment is conducive to life and growth, or whether the environment defeats life. People within the congregational system may not be so quick to realize what a serious problem they have. The long-time leaders know that it seems to be harder each year to keep the doors open. "Why aren't more new people coming into our church?" they wonder. "And the new people who come don't have enough commitment to become leaders," they complain. But is the problem really lack of commitment on the part of the newer people? A congregation struggling to find enough leaders will benefit from looking at factors that create the congregational climate. What is there about the way the congregation carries out its life that either discourages or encourages the development of Spirit Leaders?

Factors that Discourage Leaders

Some congregations allow negative, critical people to determine the climate of the congregation. These critical spirits speak critical words to those who try to do anything or change anything. In this climate of "carping," only the very brave or the thick-skinned try to lead.

Carping Critics

The "carpers" are not necessarily trying to do anything themselves. Their personal mission statement seems to be, "defending the status quo by defeating the different."

Sally, a new member of the diaconate, is asked to chair the deacons group. She decides to change the way deacons are scheduled. She believes that it will be easier for deacons to remember when they are serving if she schedules a team for a month at a time rather than scheduling a different team to serve every Sunday.

When Wilma sees the schedule in the bulletin, she angrily confronts Sally in the hall before the worship service. "What do you mean by scheduling me for every Sunday next month? I may not be able to be here every Sunday. And that's not the way we do things here!" Sally may need to learn some leadership skills such as communicating with people who will be affected by a change before the change is implemented. But Wilma's angry confrontation only serves to discourage Sally. When other deacons also complain about the new schedule, Sally's spirit wilts in the climate of carping. She says to herself, "This is the last time I'll try to do anything in this church."

When Sally resigns as a deacon, an elder calls Sally to ask if anything is wrong. Sally talks about her discouragement with trying to improve the functioning of the deacons. The elder says, "Some people always complain about anything new. You just have to humor them." Evidently for years the leaders of the congregation have tolerated the carping instead of challenging it. This long-term leader was actually trying to teach the newer leader the congregation's dysfunction. But Sally doesn't see why she should have to humor people who discourage others with their complaints. She decides she wants to use her time and energy in a more productive way. She starts looking for another church.

It is easy for leaders to confuse conveying the unconditional love and grace of God with tolerating behavior that is destructive to the church community and to its mission. It is also easy to confuse people's "right" to express their opinions with a pattern of behavior that is consistently hurtful to others in the congregation. Add to this confusion the human tendency to fear and avoid confrontation. Then negative people are given free reign to block congregational growth and the development of new leaders. A few consistently negative people can create a congregational climate of carping.

Cowardly Communication

Cowardly communication also discourages leaders. John is hurt by a comment Bob made about him in a meeting. Instead of talking with Bob about the incident, John talks with Steve, Sue, Jerry, and Elaine. Steve takes it upon himself to say something to Bob. "Bob, a lot of people are upset by the way you conduct meetings," says Steve. This comment catches Bob by surprise, and he asks, "Who is upset and why?" "I'm not at liberty to say," says Steve. "I just thought you should know."

This is not an example of constructive criticism. It is an example of cowardly communication. John needed to talk directly with Bob, but found it easier to seek solace for his hurt feelings in talking with other people. He chose a sympathetic audience in talking with the people also put off by Bob's gruff manner. Steve felt "heroic" in bringing the matter of people being upset to Bob's attention. But Steve also engaged in cowardly communication by not taking responsibility for his words. Bob was left not knowing who was upset or why or what to do about it. Bob is discouraged and resigns his leadership position.

A Vision Void

Another discouraging factor is lack of overall vision for the congregation. People who have leadership gifts are often asked to take charge of some area of the congregation's life without the congregation having an overall direction in which the body is moving. Leaders need to know how the area they are working in or the project they are developing helps fulfill the mission of the entire congregation. Without a coherent vision…

1. energies of leaders go in many different directions and produce little benefit;
2. leaders feel like they are competing with each other for the available resources;
3. leaders are more vulnerable to the attacks of the forces in the congregation that are opposed to change.

It is important for the leader creating waves of change to be able to say, "We are not making this change for change's sake. We are not making this change because I or a few other people want it. We are changing because the congregation has a vision we believe to be from God, and moving toward the vision requires this change."

Two Graces

In facing the factors that discourage Spirit Leaders, we'd also like to offer some insights about two God-given graces that can help leaders break through to God's Easter victory: the power of spiritual agreement and an elemental understanding of spiritual warfare.

Spiritual Agreement

Church people are intimately familiar with the power that a vocal minority can exert when they pool their negative thoughts. Such negative spirits simply gang up on those who are trying to initiate a positive response to the constant demand upon churches to change to meet the shifting needs with the unchanging gospel. Negative voices sometimes seem to multiply and magnify in the dark, especially if unchallenged.

Jesus gave his followers a word to counteract this malignant influence. In Matthew 18:19–20, he states, "if two of you agree on earth about anything you ask, it will be done for you by my Father in heaven. For where two or three of you are gathered in my name, I am there among them." Of course, to claim this promise for something selfish, like maybe winning the lottery (even if you promise to tithe it!), is probably not what Jesus had in mind. This is a reference to the concentrated spiritual power brought to bear in those rare places where God's people pray according to God's purposes for God's will to be done on earth as God's will is already so fully done in the realm of heaven.

This is a prayer that unfolds around a conversation based on spiritual discernment. In this conversation leaders share their Spirit-inspired visions of what their collective situation might unfold to look like if God's will were to be done—right then and there, in time and space—as it is always being done in the eternal realm. Binding our prayerful hearts in solemn agreement for God's will to be done unleashes God's power to be applied as joyfully in the temporal realm as in the eternal realm. This is essentially another form of something most Disciple congregations are very familiar with: praying the Lord's Prayer. A prayer of agreement simply seeks to bring to bear the power of the Lord's Prayer for "God's Kingdom to come on earth as it is in heaven" to the immediate and specific situation at hand.

At a medium-sized congregation in the Midwest, a widespread feeling of easy comfortableness settled in. The leadership shared no general agreement about "Why this feeling now?" or what this might mean. Consequently, not everyone thought, "Something needs to be done to keep us from resting on our laurels." The elders were split in their discernment over whether this lull meant it was time for a quick next step in their master plan, a step that would include building additional facilities. To some, it was so obvious that "any organization that doesn't keep moving forward will slide backwards." Others believed, "Our money ought to go to outreach and missions, period!" Resistance began to build and split into factions as discussion grew more heated.

Rather than bringing in a consultant at this stage, some Spirit Leaders offered the possibility of prayer, which drew embarrassed laughter! "Well, we've tried everything else, why not prayer?" With much unspoken reluctance, they sort of "backed into" a season of intentional prayer and fasting. They joked: "Fast food we know about, but we're not sure of the nutritional value of fasting as a means for discernment!"

As an ad hoc group of congregational leaders gathered twice a week over a thirty-day period to explore the idea of fasting, they discovered how the practice can whet one's appetite for God and create longing in the human heart for God's purpose and will. Their longing for more of God's full love and power to reign in their midst personally and emerge corporately began to bring more focused discernment. Fasting sharpened their appreciation of the psalmist's words: "O taste and see that the LORD is good" (Ps. 34:8a). They realized that there are seasons of simply "being with God" in a thankful mind. Nothing has to "happen." They were also able to own up to the fact that plain "enjoying God" in worship and in administrative church life made them quite uncomfortable, perhaps because they were all trained to prefer "doing." The group named their spirit of fear that was driving the compulsion to "do something!" They balanced this insight with the practical realization that they simply did not know enough about the life cycles of their congregation. Gaining such knowledge would require further study in the near future. Meanwhile, the season of fasting and prayer brought a glad freedom and a sense of inner permission to more fully enjoy God.

Certainly not all disagreements and resistances to change are resolved so successfully in our congregational life! Just as sure as believers begin to pray in faith for God's will to be done, the divine answer to that prayer requires that other wills be undone. And when that begins to actually happen, guess what? One thing will happen for sure: opposition! This brings us to a conversation that Disciples are loathe to acknowledge as necessary: spiritual warfare.

Spiritual Warfare

Mere mention of this phrase sends some church folks into "hyper-hieroglyphics"...which is another way of saying there is no single language to talk about this subject without doing some heavy translation work. While some may speak of literally casting out demons and rebuking evil spirits, we have found talking about this in terms of understanding the dynamics of resistance in systemic analysis is another helpful language. Dr. Fred Craddock once said that Disciples have two problems when it comes to talking about the devil. Some think there is no such thing as evil—that it is merely a matter of poor social conditioning—while others "see a Beelzebub behind every bush!" Certainly some churches do manipulate with fear and label any opposition to "their ideas" as "of the devil" and a matter for "spiritual warfare."

The critical thing here is to note that the blatant abuse of this biblical concept does not negate the spiritual reality alluded to in Paul's Ephesians letter: "For our struggle is not against enemies of flesh and blood, but against the rulers, against the authorities, against the cosmic powers of the present darkness, against the spiritual forces of evil in the heavenly places" (Eph. 6:12; see also following verses). This is simply to say there are times when all our systems of analysis fail to yield insight into the true nature of the problem and no carefully reasoned intervention strategy seems to make a dent. In these moments, we turn in prayer in whatever language works best in that particular circumstance. The essential matter is to acknowledge the dynamic of opposition in the spiritual realm when we sense its occurrence and to pray, earnestly and unceasingly.

The first step in this discernment process may well be fierce self-examination. We need to ask ourselves the hard question: Could it be that *we* are the ones who have not yet "cast the beam out of our own eye"? This may help explain why we continue to project the dark shadow of the problem upon "those bad people who happen to disagree with us."

Disciples often find in the language of psychology a useful tool to help name and get at the dark dynamics of spiritual warfare. While we may not like the devil-talk and recognize the danger of shadow projection and scapegoating, we need not be naïve about spiritual powers opposed to God's victory in the world through Christ. Given the positive power God has unleashed in the world through Easter, is it any wonder that resurrection has its detractors, both in and out of the church?

Perhaps some examples drawn from watching congregations face opposition and struggle without the tools a Spirit Leader needs to engage this battle would help shed light on a few of the dynamics of resistance.

It is heartbreaking to see a new congregation struggle to get off the ground, encountering obstacles and battles while the leaders have little training and almost no theological grounding in how to understand and counter the opposition on a spiritual level.

The core leadership of one "new church" launch team could not imagine why they were having all kinds of fits getting "off the ground," and why all manner of obstacles were thrown up by certain members of their own new church team. Group prayer and spiritual discernment revealed a portion of this team was not so much excited about reaching spiritual seekers as seeking to get away from a former church that held bitter memories for them. Because they had not spent any energy grieving and healing the pain of previous church wounding, they reacted negatively to almost every "out of the box" idea proposed. This wet blanketing kept the flight ceiling too low for proper take-off!

When these dynamics were named and discussed in the group, no ownership of the problem was acknowledged; and no relinquishment of the hurt and chaos forthcoming. This open wound in the midst of their core, in their collective soul as a group, kept sabotaging legitimate efforts to reach out and welcome new seekers into the fellowship. The unconscious dynamic of repeating the sequences of wounding without much insight, much less any accountability for this chaos, simply left the pastoral staff little choice but to "un-invite" some people from serving on the launch team. How very *un*-Disciple! We are such a democratic church, right? How dare "they" and who do "they" think "they" are? The fallout was nearly unbearable.

However, this decision was reluctantly reached on the basis of the fact that the entire team was not in spiritual agreement. They understood this phase to describe the dynamic that their collective motives, attitudes, and prayers were not all lined up and pointing in the same direction. This alignment was a critical piece of working hand-to-hand and heart-to-heart to an intensely focused purpose: to bring searching souls to God's heart. The sponsoring agencies were wise enough to support the pastoral staff as they made this discernment and stuck with it, though it made for tough sledding.

The pastoral staff was sustained by a biblical image from, of all places, the book of Revelation–specifically 12:1–12, which describes a woman in the agony of labor, precarious and vulnerable as she brought forth a child, who was endangered by a dragon ready to devour the new birth. However, God snatched away the child from the dragon. Enraged at being thwarted, the dragon brought down war. Michael the Archangel battled on behalf of the beleaguered saints who were being accused and oppressed, badgered and threatened.

Perhaps it was the vicious, insistent quality to the stinging accusations heaped on the pastoral staff that helped the whole launch team catch a glimpse of the idea they were engaged in something beyond mere "personality differences." Quite often, spiritual warfare may occur simultaneously on multivalenced and multifaceted and multilayered levels. Jesus warned of the necessity of keeping our souls clean and whole but also of not allowing spiritual emptiness to overtake us, lest we be vulnerable the influence of evil powers (Lk. 11:14–26). To their credit, the pastors made no wild counteraccusations about their accusers being "evil." They chose the path of persistence in prayer, quietly invoking the name of Jesus as described in the same chapter of Luke. Their quiet confidence in the power of God to sustain a work born of God won the day and allowed the launch team to experience a resurrection of their own!

The basic principles of spiritual agreement are not necessarily established through a checklist of specific techniques or methods. We have found that the practice of communal silent prayer and reflective conversation often allows a strong common purpose to emerge that may be named as holy; one worthy of sacrifice, risk, and uncommon boldness. Once this holy purpose is named in the midst and claimed by each person in their own way, expressing allegiance and commitment, all the group's energies can be aimed at the emergence of this purpose. Here is where tangents are tested, stray thoughts redirected, goals retargeted, and energies awry may be reaimed. Now all activity and thought are directed toward the fulfillment of God's will as this group has come to understand it.

Spiritual purpose that emerges through the practice of meditating on scripture and prayer accompanied by seeing the light of God in the heart of each other is a powerful binding force in the spiritual realm. This kind of voluntary allegiance pledged and devoted to the confession of holy purpose in the name of

Jesus and for the sake of the reign of God is quite impossible to shake! Didn't Jesus say: "the gates of Hades will not prevail against it" (Mt. 16:18b)?

Just to help bring this conversation back to Earth, let's remember that sometimes we can get all caught up in imagining recalcitrant opposition as some "demonic barrier" related to evil forces. Often the fact of the matter is, we are up against a situation in which clear boundaries of appropriate behavior are being violated and we have to hold to some old-fashioned, "real time" accountability.

A floundering suburban congregation decided to create a small training group to enhance both spiritual growth and, in turn, attract seekers with the intimate joy of practicing everyday faith and support of each other's journey. The expressed hope was that each member would eventually start their own group for the same purpose. These groups would be developed in the same open-hearted, trusting, welcoming spirit. This wonderful vision for discipleship growth was nearly destroyed when it became known that one person in the group was using the spiritually intimate setting of the group as an occasion to sexually proposition members.

In a misguided effort to "protect" what was viewed as a fragile and critical project as well as a fragile personality, the group tolerated this inappropriate behavior way too long. When the pastor learned of the destructive dynamics, she and a male elder confronted this predator and forced him to leave the group to undergo intensive therapy, pending criminal charges that were held pending until it was clear that his therapeutic compliance was forthcoming.

While such antisocial behavior was naively tolerated in the name of charity, it nearly devastated a small group renewal movement that, after these shaky beginnings, eventually became the core for this congregation's spiritual revitalization. It is scary to contemplate how close this congregation came to totally losing the trust level and morale of their church in an attempt to protect the bad behavior of one individual whose sickness had to be named and challenged before healing could begin to take place for him and for the congregation he tried to plunder. It is a good thing to discover that appropriate limits can work, if leaders can be bold enough to act courageously. Spiritual agreement and spiritual warfare must be practiced at times to defeat negative forces hindering a church's mission.

Factors That Encourage Leaders

If a congregation desires to improve the climate for leaders, the first step is seeking a vision from God for their identity and mission. Vision is a compelling picture of the future toward which God is inviting them.

Seeking God's Vision

The congregation can engage in a prayerful process of discerning who God is calling them to be and what God is calling them to do. (A guide for such a prayer process is offered in appendix 2 of this book.) The process can result in clear direction for the congregation. The leaders can then prayerfully set direction for their area or project in line with the overall direction of the congregation. Vision provides a measure for determining which proposals and ideas will be implemented. When they share a common vision, leaders can cooperate in the wise stewardship of resources.

The climate of a congregation whose building was located in a neighborhood changing from suburban to inner city could best be described as "cranky." Everyone in the church noticed that fewer people filled the chairs on Sunday mornings, and that the church struggled each month to pay the bills. The church treasurer was very "cranky." The chair of the evangelism committee fought with the chair of the worship committee about whether the memorial money given for "church growth" should go toward advertising or new hymnals. As the fight went on, the tone of church meetings got crankier. The lay leaders tried to understand why the church was declining instead of growing and looked for someone to blame.

Placing the blame on the minister was an obvious thing to do. Under increasing attack, the minister became cranky and blamed the lay leaders. How could he move the church forward with people who had so little understanding of the faith and so little commitment? His counterattacks resulted in crankier lay leaders. People in the congregation who didn't really know about all the attacks and counterattacks only knew they dreaded coming to church. They "hung in" out of a sense of duty, but they felt discontent and were often ungracious and prickly with one another.

The grace and power of God broke into this climate of crankiness when the minister and the elders went on a weekend retreat together. They spent hours praying together. They asked God to show them how to move from their stuck place into the future God has for them. They talked about the needs of the community and realized they really didn't know who lived in the area around the church. They shared their individual hopes and dreams for the church and then concluded their retreat by offering their ideas to God and opening themselves to receive God's plans for the church's future.

In the next months the minister and elders led the church in finding out more about their community. Leaders obtained and studied demographic information. They prayer-walked the neighborhoods around the church building. They talked with people who lived and worked there. The leaders began talking about the neighborhood as "the church's mission field." They became aware of many unchurched families with small children in their "mission field." As they listened for the voice of God in the midst of the voices around them, they grew excited about developing ministries for families with small children. They listened to the voice of their own lives through the excitement and energy they felt around this vision. They claimed and celebrated this new vision.

But what about implementing the vision with their limited resources?

Through the months of seeking direction from God, the minister realized that he was not a good "fit" for this congregation, especially with their new vision. He also knew that his salary (low as it was) consumed 80 percent of the congregation's financial resources. He listened to his own life and felt the nudge to find a ministry setting where his teaching gift could be more fully utilized. He submitted his resignation with the proposal that the congregation hire a part-time minister, gifted to reach young families. He further proposed that the congregation hire a part-time worship leader to help the congregation move into a style of worship better meeting the needs of younger people. "There may even be enough money to hire a part-time person to develop ministries with children," he said. Although some members reacted to the resignation with sadness, most felt the minister's proposals were "right on." A prayerful search process resulted in the hiring of a young couple with gifts to lead the congregation in developing a new style of worship *and* in developing children's ministries!

The minister stayed long enough to help orient the new couple. He had the joy of feeling the climate of the congregation changing for the better before he left. "I no longer have a headache after the morning worship service," said one of the leaders. "I actually look forward to coming to church now," said another. The church treasurer even looked less worried as the weeks went by. Soon after the minister left, the congregation called a part-time bi-vocational minister who had evangelistic gifts as well as leadership skills. "I guess our approach has been a little unconventional," says an elder. "We discovered that God is waiting to give new vision for those who are willing to get out of the boxes they are trapped in. A common vision helps us in so many ways."

Constructive Communication

Constructive communication in a congregation is a great encouragement factor. Constructive communication is based on the passage in Matthew's gospel in which Jesus instructs his disciples to speak directly with one another when there is hurt or disagreement: "If another member of the church sins against you, go and point out the fault when the two of you are alone" (Mt. 18:15). Constructive communication requires that we take responsibility for what we say to one another. We don't dump vague complaints like, "Some people are upset," on each other. If we are upset with something another person in the church has done, we talk only with that person about the offense. Before we go to that person, we ask for God's guidance. Is this worth talking about, or do we simply need to forgive, release it, and move forward? If it is worth talking about, we pray the result will be ultimately helpful to everyone involved before we engage in the conversation.

The minister of a struggling church met with the elders to talk about the health of the congregation. "A congregation needs to be healthy before it can grow," said the minister. "One of our major health issues is the way we communicate with each other. People talk *about* other people, but they don't talk directly *to* other people. I'm suggesting that we as the spiritual leaders pray for healthier communication and that we model it." After some discussion, the leaders decided they themselves would seek to follow Matthew 18:15 in their relationships in the congregation. They outlined a procedure they would follow when someone came to them with a complaint about someone else in the church. The procedure included the following questions:

1. Have you talked directly with the person you are upset with?
2. May I go with you to talk with the person?
3. If you are not willing to talk with the person, no more should be said about the issue.

An elder named Maryanne soon had opportunity to work with the procedure. Paula came to her with a complaint about Susan's children running around the church unsupervised whenever Susan was at the church. "Can't she keep her kids from dragging stuff out of the cabinets in the Sunday school rooms?" asked Paula.

Maryanne asked the first question according to the procedure. "Have you talked with Susan about this and why it concerns you?"

"Well, it's not just me!" said Paula defensively. "Lots of people are upset about her kids."

"But have you talked with Susan to let her know how it creates difficulty for you when her kids pull stuff out of the cabinets?"

"I don't really think it's my place to talk with her. I think the elders should handle this," said Paula.

Maryanne moved to the second question of the procedure. "Would it help if I went with you to talk with Susan about this issue?"

Paula paused and thought about this possibility. "Oh," she said, "I guess we do have to tolerate a certain amount of mess from kids if we want young families involved in the congregation."

Maryanne saw that Paula had decided not to take responsibility for dealing with this issue. She went on to step 3 of the procedure. "Since you've decided this issue is not important enough for a conversation with Susan, it would be best not to talk with anyone else about it." Paula reacted in surprise. She was not used to being held accountable for honest and direct communication. She went off in a huff. But Maryanne believed her response to Paula was constructive communication and was a contribution toward congregational health.

Within several months the elders were challenged to follow the procedure they outlined for others. In their continuing conversation about congregational health they identified several people in the church who were consistently critical and negative.

"I heard Bill angrily complaining to the minister about the changes in the worship service," said an elder. "And this was in front of first-time guests."

"Bill has been a thorn in the side of every minister we've had for the past twenty years," said another elder.

"Are we going to talk with Bill about his behavior and the damage it does in the life of the church?" asked the minister. "I didn't have the opportunity in the setting right after worship to really talk with Bill. I think the conversation would have more impact if one of you elders went with me to talk with Bill."

The elders discussed the possibility of this conversation alienating Bill, who was one of the biggest contributors to the church. "We've tolerated behaviors in this church that wouldn't be tolerated anywhere else because we've been so afraid of losing someone," said Maryanne. "I think we need to do what it takes to get healthier, even if we risk losing someone. I'll go with the minister to talk with Bill."

The minister and Maryanne made an appointment with Bill. The minister expressed how Bill's continual criticism discouraged her. She said she was available to listen to Bill's suggestions, but his angry criticism on Sunday morning in front of a guest was unacceptable. Bill launched into an angry tirade, concluding with his usual threat to leave the church.

Maryanne calmly said, "The elders are in agreement that this kind of behavior is unacceptable. Bill, we love you, and we don't want you to leave. We're all trying to change so that the congregation can grow. We ask that you pray about this and work with us to create a healthier climate in our church."

After the visit, Bill stayed away from the congregation for almost a year. Bill told members who called about how the minister and Maryanne had offended him. Some members thought the elders should apologize to Bill. But the elders and minister stood together in their covenant to do what they could to promote constructive communication in the congregation. They explained that challenging in love the people whose actions consistently blocked growth was part of their ministry as Spirit Leaders. Bill did eventually come back to church. Everyone warmly welcomed him. He still manifested a critical spirit from time to time, but he no longer raised his voice in angry criticism in a public setting.

Intentional Mentoring

A very important factor in congregations with a good climate for leader development is intentional mentoring. In these congregations Spirit Leaders who are currently serving look for emerging leaders and spend time with them. The mentoring leaders invite mutual sharing of spiritual journeys. They find out about the gifts and interests of the emerging leaders. They invite emerging leaders to join them in the ministries they are doing in and through the congregation. If the emerging leaders are especially interested in those ministries, the mentoring leaders provide hands-on training, inviting the emerging leaders to do more and more as they feel ready.

Lee was a mentoring leader. He loved the ministry of taking communion to people who were homebound or hospitalized on Sunday afternoons. But rarely did Lee do this ministry alone. He often took a teenager or young adult from the church with him. He shared his love for serving in this way and gave the younger persons hands-on training as they made the visits with him. Lee used the time in the car before and after visits to find out about the emerging leader and to share faith stories. When he found a young person who seemed especially interested in the ministry of visiting, Lee encouraged the young person to do more of the talking and praying with each visit they made together. Mentoring leaders also help emerging leaders discover their own God-dreams and help them turn the dreams into reality.

Even basically healthy congregations have power dynamics that the person new to the system may not know. The new leader in the congregation may not know who the key players are or how to get things done in the congregational system. Longer-term leaders who know the system can help make way for newer leaders by advocating for them.

A pastor who had only been in a congregation for a couple of years greatly appreciated one of his elders named George, who had been in the congregation for years and understood the system well. Whenever the pastor had an idea, he talked it over with George. Sometimes George pointed out why the idea would not work or why it was not the time to try the idea. But often George identified the best way to get the idea implemented. George identified the people who needed to support the idea for it to gain acceptance. He talked with these "influencers" over lunch or on the golf course, helping them to see the merit of the minister's idea. George influenced the influencers more effectively than the minister could. Spirit Leaders who have power in a congregational system can pave the way for leaders who do not have power. Spirit Leaders encourage new leaders by advocating for them.

Conclusion

The climate of the congregation to a large degree controls the future of the congregation. If the climate is kept unhealthy through factors such as critical carping, cowardly communication, and vision void, current leaders will become discouraged, and new leaders will not emerge. In fact, the congregation will stagnate and eventually die because new people will not be attracted to an unhealthy body. If you have realized that the climate of your congregation is not healthy, take heart! God provides two powerful means of breaking destructive patterns, confronting evil behaviors, and promoting spiritual health and wholeness for the body. These two graces are "praying in agreement" and "conducting spiritual warfare." Engaging in these graces is what we can do. Release from spiritual bondage, healing, and transformation is what the Spirit of God does. Take heart! Your congregation can become healthy and can become a sign of hope. Much depends on what the current leaders of your congregation decide to do.

Questions for Reflection

1. What words or images come to mind as you describe the climate of your congregation?
2. As a leader, what factors in congregational life have discouraged you? encouraged you? Where do you go with this?
3. What *one* thing could current leaders of your congregation do that would vastly improve the climate for emerging leaders?

4. How can the current leaders of your congregation provide support for emerging leaders?
5. What is a concern in the life of your congregation around which a group might seek agreement in prayer?
6. Is "spiritual warfare" a term that describes anything you've experienced?
7. Do you think it is the responsibility of Christian leaders to confront people whose behavior threatens the well-being of others in the congregation? If so, what guidelines might help guide these moments of accountability?

The Training of a Spirit Leader

We are such weenies when it comes to discipleship! For decades Disciples have been overwrought with the philosophy that if we make following Jesus too hard, no one will sign up to follow. The fact of the matter is, the opposite proves true. Church people are not at all stupid, not even a little bit! They know when leaders say, "Oh just accept the job! Let me put your name down to fill that slot. No problem, it will be easy!" Church folks innately know that if discipleship really were that easy, we wouldn't have gotten so far as asking them!

As counterintuitive as it may seem, once people connect their reason for serving Christ with the call of God upon their life, the assignment's degree of difficulty becomes infinitely less critical. We have witnessed believers go to extraordinary lengths once they realize their commitment matters to the heart of God. The training of Spirit Leaders takes on new energies when we honestly admit: This will not be easy, but it matters eternally. People get that!

Having explored the discipleship methods for training Spirit Leaders (whatever they may be called in different denominations), we have come to what may seem a strange conclusion. While there are critical elements in each model, almost any approach that includes them will work, *if* the leaders will work it! Effectiveness seems to be less a function of "getting all the proper methods and techniques of doing it right" and more a focus on doing a few of the right things.

One example might be found in First Christian Church of Frankfort, Kentucky's "Training of the Twelve." This year-long experience in discipleship and spiritual leadership evolved to help form the basis for the Bethany Project, a pilot project for modeling spiritual leadership renewal on a national scale, offered to Disciples recently through the Office of the General Minister and President.

Training of the Twelve seeks to create a safe and trusting spiritual community in which God's call upon one's life may be explored. It is not rocket science. It is certainly not an original idea or even a novel concept. Gathering a small circle of potential leaders and training them, intimately and personally, over a period of time in the art of Christian discipleship and discernment, then turning them loose to lead, worked for Jesus. Maybe that's all the endorsement we need.

T-12 was born out of a continuous spiritual struggle to come to grips with God's honest truth: No congregation will ever rise above the commitment level of its leadership. For good or ill, it is so. If we, as Spirit Leaders, are not willing to be regularly challenged to practice the practices of faith and live out of the integrity of who we are before God in our faith community, the church *cannot* rise above its present level. There seems to be no way around this truth. In the realm of the Spirit, this is how the principle seems to operate.

The authors encountered these principles "up close and personal" in the ministry of Dr. Herman Norton, dean of Disciples House at Vanderbilt Divinity School. Dr. Norton was a powerful figure in leadership circles. He served in the ranks of Army chaplaincy, from which he retired as a general. He taught at Vanderbilt as professor of American church history and was a strong "behind-the-scenes" leader in the Vanderbilt Faculty Senate. Anyone who knew Dr. Norton clearly got the picture of a man who eschewed the slightest hint of piety! Yet he was utterly devoted to his God-calling.

Judy and I were just two of hundreds of students he mentored through seminary studies. We each slowly realized that the measure of faith he aspired for his seminarians to achieve was also the measure of faith (and beyond) that he personally practiced. His personal sacrifices to educate and finance the lives of leaders-in-training are as indelible as his handwriting was illegible! His "Spirit Leader" example was always without fanfare, and his generosity quite secretive.

Decades have passed since Dr. Norton's days as the dean who educated a generation of Vanderbilt Disciples ministers; yet his leadership legacy left a powerful impact. His life and ministry demonstrate the power of a dedicated leader to raise the level of expectation.

Believing that personal example and setting the standard high are leadership principles that directly apply to improving the spiritual quality of parish life, I began to seek out small arenas of influence where these principles could be effectively practiced. I soon realized many of the leaders I was trying to recruit for key leadership positions were appropriately reluctant. Being competent in their own fields of endeavor, they assumed mastery of a body of basic theological knowledge would be necessary to lead in church settings, just as it would be in any other field for which they were not trained. Whenever I was able to convince a leader otherwise ("Just love the Lord and jump in there and lead, no previous experience or special training is necessary"), the results were disastrous both for them and for the congregation.

Out of the ashes of such painful failures, the vision for T-12 arose. T-12 is a crash course, offered over a year's time to twelve persons, who covenant to meet for ninety minutes a week, hold the conversations in total confidence, pray for one another, encourage each other's spiritual gifts, discern their calling, and serve in some ministry of God's calling. The atmosphere created is something I often call "an uproarious combination of prayer meeting, potluck, and personal therapy."

The session begins with instruction on how to create and share your personal spiritual autobiography. Two participants get twenty minutes apiece to tell the story of what it is like to be "who they are" with God and to trace the milestones of their journeys. Circle prayers for their continued spiritual growth follow behind a season of positive bombardment.

Once every group member has presented a spiritual autobiography, the group's energy in the sessions shifts to center on each person's S.H.A.P.E[1]...that is: Spiritual Gifts, Heart for God, Abilities, Personality, and Experience. While the entire S.H.A.P.E. resource is worked through and discussed, the major block of energy centers on spiritual gifts. This focus centers on the recognition that we can't do Christ's work without Christ's Spirit, who is manifested among us through spiritual gifts.

Another key ingredient is a thorough grounding in practicing the practices of our faith. T-12ers learn *lectio divina,* centering prayer, scripture meditation, prayer walking, fasting, journaling, devotional quiet time, healing, Sabbath, bibliotherapy, spiritual agreement, and dealing with resistance in the spiritual realm. They were not just talking "about" these disciplines. They actually took time to experience each practice and then as a group reflect on that practice. These elements gave the group a common grounding in the basic ways leaders sustain their faith when those around them appear to be losing theirs. This ability to know how to get to those places where the spiritual food is and to feed oneself and sustain one's soul in the company of others—these are the essential ingredients in becoming a spiritual eagle and not remaining a "baby bird."

A thorough review of the flow of the basic story line of the Bible comes next. Biblical facts are referenced and arranged for easier recollection. The major block of time centers on a study of

---

[1]The S.H.A.P.E. acronym is more fully explored in a privately published booklet available through First Christian Church, Frankfort. The booklet is a workbook/resource that details the multifaceted self-study. Through a series of inventories and questionnaires the inner S.H.A.P.E. of each person's discipleship is elicited, explored, and affirmed in the context of loving Christian community.

the life of Christ, with much discussion around "meeting Jesus again for the first time." (This phrase, which titles a book by Marcus Borg book, is actually a line from Thomas Merton's prayer journal.) Some years, T-12 participants prepare and present biographical sketches of each of the twelve disciples in the Bible to learn about the variety of styles we follow in faith. Other years they may select the life of a saint, identifying and demonstrating the characteristics of Christ's life that shine through the saint's life.

Parallel to conversation around nurturing the relationship with Christ, they begin to review a variety of visionary church leaders. Perspectives include leaders from Lyle Schaller to Bill Easum and Tom Bandy, from Len Sweet to George Barna and George Bullard, to emerging church leaders and beyond. This exposure to cutting-edge leadership ideas stirs lots of questions and engenders lively discussion. At about this point in the process, some sort of road-trip is organized. This helps solidify in the minds of the participants what some of these ideas might look like when practiced in a real live church setting. Some years, we attend a workshop at a famous church. Other years, we have offered a retreat called "Journey to Bethany," developed in cooperation with Rev. Harold Goodwin, retired senior minister of Decatur Trinity Church in Memphis. This is a Disciple version of the now famous spiritual formation retreat experience called "Emmaus Walk," offered originally through the United Methodists' Upper Room.[2] Whatever the out-of-town event may be, there is something about traveling together that seems to integrate a lot of learning and also make for spiritual bonding within the group life.

---

[2]If you are interested in experiencing the "Journey to Bethany" spiritual retreat, it is currently offered annually at Lindenwood Christian Church. You may contact Rev. Harold Goodwin at Lindenwood Christian Church in Memphis, Tennessee, for full information about this retreat and renewal experience. Briefly, it is a scaled-down forty-hour version of the more elaborate Emmaus Walk renewal experience. This model is thoroughly grounded in Disciples theology.

The group focus then shifts to a complete review of all the major Christian doctrines. This leaves most participants groaning, because it is technical, detailed, and carefully referenced biblically. During the review, participants complain ad nauseam and brag about surviving the snoozing induced by boring facts. Later, they seem to find that small neurons fire and close mental synapses, which help them actually recall the core truths of the faith and discover the ability to articulate and apply these core truths for themselves. The results are stunning in terms of theological literacy.

As this intense experience winds toward a close, we begin a thorough review of the work of Robert Greenleaf on servant leadership. Everyone is asked to answer these questions: "What would it look like for me to adapt these central principles to my own discipleship as a life-long practice? What shifts and changes would be required for me to make this a way of life? What will be my leadership legacy? Where is God calling me to serve as a servant leader?" We like to modify some of Greenleaf's focus to ask the question: "Regardless of what my specific leadership assignment may (or may not be) at any particular season in my life with this community of faith, how is God calling me through this T-12 experience to serve as a life-long Spirit Leader? What does this calling mean, and what shape does this take in my own life?"

When the T-12 group "graduates," they are commissioned in worship and begin work in some area of the church's life of their choosing and God's calling. Many of the T-12 groups continue to meet at least monthly for prayer and support as they carry out their vital ministries as Spirit Leaders. Can you imagine the focused spiritual energy these communities of faith contribute daily to the larger body of Christ?

Hearing the Challenge and the Invitation

After potential T-12ers learn the basic outline of the expectations, the comment most often heard is: "So when are we supposed to find time to do anything else?"

Maybe a good reply might be: "What do you think you are doing that matters more than this?" Actually, this is where the stretching of faith we talked about earlier in this chapter comes into play, because potential Spirit Leaders are tired of being told, "Just sign up, it's easy." They long to hear: "This will be the spiritual challenge of your life, but with the challenge comes the faith to meet it!"

Challenge to the Leaders of Spiritual Leaders

If you have not yet identified the next Spirit Leaders in your community of faith, claimed them through prayerful discernment, called them by faith, and begun training them, may we respectfully ask: What else are you doing that is so all-fired important?

Okay, caring for the dying. But our churches are dying from the lack of spiritual leadership. If you know how to lead them in the Spirit and yet find yourself captured by the insistent demands of lesser priorities…fear not! God will still have a Spirit witness in this world…it just won't be through congregations of the Disciples of Christ!

This may sound too radical, but we are convinced that too many of our solid Spiritual Leaders of emerging Spirit Leaders are not yet to the critical point of "having done with lesser things." They are not yet ready to push all the chips over on the claiming, calling, training, and forming of our next generation of leadership.

Are *you* as a Spiritual Leader of your Spirit Leaders stressed to the max by the press of conflicting duties? Do these duties leave you feeling so totally overwhelmed, constantly run ragged, and forever on the hairy edge of emotional exhaustion that you don't know what to do next? Then we invite you to hear this as a blessed invitation: "Stop doing what *others* can do or what you can *train* others to do! Do *only* that which God has called *you* to do!"

Consider: Is it possible that your Spirit Leaders are not free to find their calling because you are not free to find yours? If you continue to dawdle on the edges of your Spirit Leadership instead of crawling out on the hairy edge…guess what?…You are in the way of your Spirit Leaders finding their fullest spiritual destiny!

The Invitation to Leaders of Spirit Leaders

If you pray to God for the courage to follow the preceding challenge to find freedom to discover your own spiritual calling, then perhaps one of two things will happen:

1. Others will begin to sense a new urgency to pick up the slack when you stop duplicating their callings so that you can do what only you can do.
2. Your congregation may find (now that what you *were* doing is not being done) that maybe it wasn't as critical to the heartbeat of the mission as everybody once thought!

As a Spirit Leader of Spirit Leaders, following this invitation calls for holy boldness, but you will never regret your obedience. "God doesn't need you to be another 'Billy Graham.'" God's already got one of those (but thanks anyway). God just needs for you to be the Spirit Leader of a new generation of Spirit Leaders that God has called you to be.

If you will put your hand on your heart and promise this obedience, it may please God to use your boldness to raise up, out of some unknown, out-of-the-way place, the next Esther or Moses, Lydia or Peter, Timothy or Phoebe!

Conclusion

There is no "neatly packaged ten-week program," or nifty, thrifty organizational solution to the call for Spirit Leaders. Yet we can seek to practice an unending, open-ended radical openness to the Spirit's leading. If we will courageously and continually practice this, we will know the grace described in Thomas Merton's prayer "The Road Ahead," of God's leading "by the right road, though I may know nothing about it."[1]

Leadership is not "function" extrapolated from certain organizational principles. It is a life-style, a way of being before God, a chosen path of life. The church no longer enjoys the luxury of training leaders and then warehousing them until needed. We must train them on the fly, and they will have to fly...now!

Furthermore, these younger Spirit Leaders will need to make choices about their own deeply divided inner spiritual loyalties. Sooner or later, Spirit Leaders return to the crossroads and make a choice about their own "road less traveled" that makes all the difference. This calls for those who would lead to make a Rosa Parks type of decision. One day, Rosa rode home on the bus,

---

[1]Thomas Merton, *Thoughts in Solitude* (New York: Farrar, Straus, & Cudahy, 1958), 83.

bone weary from work. The bus driver demanded that she go stand in the back of the bus—the "Black" section—where no seats were available, even though there were plenty of seats in the front. In that moment, Rosa eternally decided: " I will no longer live in a way that contradicts my most deeply held beliefs," and sat down. This was the turning point for Rosa Parks, and for Spirit Leaders too.

We believe the Spirit's call during the days of General Assembly is to our current leaders who will choose to understand the rest of their life as a devotion to mentoring the younger generations of Spirit Leaders.

To put it another way, you can rest assured our "up-and-coming" leaders will get solid grounding in theology and sound, practical, tactical techniques on administration. But who will teach them that nothing substitutes for their leading out of the place they live with God? How will our future Samuels and Sarahs come to know God's voice without spiritual coaching? Who will help form them in the Spirit?

Disciples recognize the cry for leadership because our nifty little denomination is approaching the bottoming-out point.

Our human strength has proven too weak, our politics proven too partisan, and our human wisdom too shallow.

God appears to be using this moment of utter weakness to grant Disciples a chance to sing the words of an old hymn: "Rise up, O saints of God! The church for you doth wait, with strength unequal to the task; rise up and make it great."[2]

If you hear this book as a prophetic call for this rising, you have heard it right!

If you hear this book as a call to let the Spirit lead, you have heard it right!

But most of all, if you hear your calling as a Spirit Leader, then you have heard what we believe the Spirit is saying to the churches!

---

[2]"Rise Up, O Saints of God!" words by William P. Merrill, 1911, no. 611 in *Chalice Hymnal* (St. Louis: Chalice Press, 1995).

The "Training of the Twelve" Course

OVERVIEW OF THE T-12 EXPERIENCE

The T-12 Mission and Expectations

The Mission of T-12

1. Give you time and a comfortable place to learn more about your gifts and your own inner life as you seriously attend the matter of your own spiritual growth.

2. Review the basic truths and teachings of the Christian faith in a fresh way and to relate the Bible and doctrine to life as you find it.

3. Experience the joy of learning, growing, sharing, praying, and journeying in a small group where trust, respect, mutuality, and love for God grow on you.

4. Provide the necessary ministry tools for a new generation of Spirit Leaders for the life and ministries of the church community and the kingdom of God.

5. Provide folks who are in major transitions in their life, work, family, and service the "blessing of the broom tree" season of Elijah (1 Kings 19)—a place of refuge and respite—to refresh, retool, regroup, reenvision, and revitalize.

What T-12 Will Ask of You

1. Hold your heart fiercely open to one another and to God. Be ready and willing to honor the work of God within your soul, as God may be moving you along from where you've been to where you yet may be.
2. Take seriously the T-12 covenant:
   a. Pray for one another daily.
   b. Hold the conversation of the group in confidence within the room; outside the room talk only about your own experience, *not* that of others; expect to challenge and be challenged to personal accountability on this matter, because trust grounds our conversation deeply in God.
   c. Attend the weekly meetings faithfully unless you face dire emergency or out-of-town work.
   d. Keep up with your reading or preparation assignments and your study buddy.
   e. Develop a personal devotional life that fits your rhythms and habits as a person.
   f. Seek to find a place of service that is located at the intersection of where your deep joy and the world's deep need meet.
3. As a T-12 alum, take a special assignment in the life of the congregation that fits your gifts and calling as you come to claim them.
4. After orientation and some careful coaching, prepare your spiritual autobiography.
5. Work with various tools for personality inventory.
6. Complete your SHAPE booklet.
7. Actively participate and share from these assignments in conversations around the table in a way that adds a positive contribution to the group's well being.

Implementing the T-12 Model

How We Do It

1. All pastoral staff are involved in various teaching assignments.

2. Recruit individuals who may be on the edge of burnout, paying attention to the spiritual passages of a person's life and the changes needed.

3. The full group understands and agrees to abide with the expectations, including weekly attendance and confidentiality of meetings, and each participant signs covenant.

4. First meeting reviews
   * personal expectations: Why T-12? Why now?
   * flow and design
   * the unusually high commitment level required, which will eventually lead individuals to participation and design of personal ministry
   * a covenant agreement, which each participant signs

5. The group sets schedule for twelve-month program, including some holiday and summer breaks.

6. The program begins with spiritual autobiographical writing, with two people (including staff) designated to share their stories each week.

7. Meetings are ninety minutes; they always start on time with a devotional moment and prayer, and always close on time with prayer dedicated to persons in need and to needs and praises arising from the meeting.

Course Outline

1. Faith Story development (8–10 weeks) with sign-up for "Journey to Bethany" retreat weekend for spiritual development modeled after Emmaus Walk program;

2. Writing and working with SHAPE booklets to discover personal spiritual shape (4–6 weeks);

3. Biblical overview on themes (Trinity or kerygma modified) (6–8 weeks);

4. Theological study (8–10 weeks);

5. Sociological context for our century (6 weeks);

6. Pastoral care/case study (6 weeks);

7. Other interests:
   * Servant Leadership study

- Faith practices and spiritual development (with quiet days and one or two one-day retreats)

Other Important Features

1. Guest speakers and trainers are used as available or appropriate.
2. T-12 alum help in training, praying for, and mentoring current participants.
3. Special communion service and quiet walk time occur, in which participants seek and share with the group the direction God is calling them in individual ministry through identified gifts, faith experiences, and spiritual journey.
4. Pastors use intentional small group design and process to teach and guide the participants.
5. Pastors devote special time in staff meetings to pray for participants.
6. As time allows, pastors are available for personal counseling, mentoring, and encouragement throughout the year to help individuals as they seek to be fully called as Christ's disciples.
7. Pastors intentionally urge and give permission for individuals to counsel with them and then to strike out on their own in their call from God to do ministry.
8. The course is designed for persons seeking a deeper spiritual journey and specific spiritual leadership training in a group of committed folks, including the pastors.
9. Meetings are held regularly in the same room, at the same time, every week, with all covenant members expected to attend every week.
10. Groups may decide they want to bring snacks for the meetings, snacks that for some groups develop into "communion food."

Summary

As you can see, this is not a strictly structured or curriculum-designed course. Generally, we change and tweak it as we move through the year or as we discover a new writing or article worth the group's investigation. All pastors resource and share the teaching, group-leading role. We cannot overemphasize that the critical piece is a leadership team who will work together to produce the meetings and to work the time factor (ninety minutes, and *only* ninety minutes, per meeting). The spiritual commitment by the pastors to the members is critical in prayer and in the group process. The pastors allow God to work through their gifts and callings to walk with the participants in the group. Only God's Spirit will lead these folks in the direction God is calling them for ministry. Pastors are not the masters of this direction, but do help in the discernment process.

THE T-12 COVENANT

Attendance: I agree to be at the session each week unless a genuine emergency arises.

Participation: I will enter enthusiastically into group discussion and sharing.

Confidentiality: I will not share with anyone outside the group the stories of those in the group.

Honesty: I will be forthright and truthful in what is said. If I do not feel that I can share something, I will say, "I pass" for that question.

Openness: I will be candid with others in appropriate ways and allow others to share for themselves.

Respect: I will not judge others, give advice, or criticize.

Care: I will be open to the needs of others in appropriate ways.

Prayer: I will pray daily for my study buddy and for all other T-12 participants.

Signed: _____

FORMAT OF SPIRITUAL AUTOBIOGRAPHY PRESENTATIONS

Presentation (20 Minutes)

This is the heart of the session—the presentation of spiritual autobiographies by *each* group member.

THE ROLE OF THE PRESENTER IS TO

- share a well-prepared spiritual autobiography
- be honest in accordance with the level of trust in the group
- be disciplined enough to end in time for discussion
- be open to the affirmation that follows

THE ROLE OF GROUP MEMBERS IS TO

- give the presenter their full attention (to listen in a focused manner is a great gift and stands in contrast to merely hearing someone)
- be affirming in their body language (how they listen helps or hinders the presenter)
- listen with the following questions in mind:
  a. What strikes you about this story? What is similar to your own experience? What is quite opposite from it? In other words, listen to that person's story in relationship to your story, seeking both points of similarity and difference, so as to provide points for the discussion.
  b. What do you learn from the story? What new insights come into focus for you?
  c. What are the unique and special features about the presenter? What special gifts do you discern in his or her life?
  d. If you made a sanctified guess, into which areas of ministry might God lead the storyteller? What might be his or her place in the work of God's kingdom?
  e. What, if anything, puzzles you in this story? What would you like to understand better?

- not interrupt (allow space for silence)
- not interpret, to not explain, correct, suggest, or criticize the life of another person.

Discussion (15 minutes)

The most common problem in a spiritual autobiography session is the lack of time to discuss what has been presented. There are various reasons for this:

- *The difficulty of any person compressing an entire life into 15 to 30 minutes.* The challenge for the presenter is to select the key issues/incidents/insights to share and to set aside others. The hardest thing is to decide what to leave out of the story.
- *The fear of judgment.* Sometimes the feeling of the presenter is, "If I use up all the time, then no one can criticize me for how I have lived." This is an unwarranted fear. For one thing, all the participants have agreed in signing the covenant "not to judge others, give advice, or criticize." For another, after hearing a person's story honestly told, our desire is not to criticize but to care.
- *Bad time management skills.* We simply forget the clock. We have so much to say. This is why the small group leaders have the task of watching the clock and reminding the presenter when time is almost up.

Leaders should conduct the discussion in the following way:

- *Begin with Affirmation.* When the presentation is finished, begin the discussion by going around the circle and asking each person to identify very briefly one element of the presentation he or she most appreciated. Continue this spirit of affirmation throughout the discussion.
- *Turn to Resonance.* Using the listening questions, discuss the story itself, including what members heard in the presentation that connects with their stories. The point of the interaction is mutual sharing and mutual discovery. We learn from one another. Often others "see" for us. We discover

that God is working in our lives by noting God's work in the lives of others.
- *Conclude with Response.* Near the end of the discussion, allow the presenter to respond. He or she may have already been doing this in the course of the interaction.

Pray (10 minutes)

The purpose of this time of prayer is to ask God's blessing on the person who has shared his or her story. This act of blessing is a great gift we can give one another.

One way the group can pray includes:

- *Affirmation*: Go around the circle and allow each person to name one thing he or she has come to appreciate about the presenter.
- *Prayer*: Spend a few moments in prayer, thanking God for the presenter and asking God to guide this person as life unfolds.
- *Blessing*: Ask God to bless this person and empower him or her to be God's person and to do God's will.

Spiritual Journaling

Journaling focuses the mind and heart by praying at the point of a pen, with the aim of discerning the presence of God amidst the path of life!

Preparing to Journal

1. Define the period of life you are currently in. When did it begin? What boundaries separate this period from previous periods?
2. Who are the key persons in this season? Are they positive or negative influences?
3. What are the distinguishing events of this period?
4. Are any key images emerging? How are you engaging them?
5. Describe your inner state and physical awarenesses.
6. What is your central prayer—your deepest desire before God in this season?
7. Can you identify hinge events, crossroads, transitional moments you are facing?
8. Do you experience any dream themes or recurring images that make sense in the light of God?

Getting Started in Journaling

1. Remember that this is not for a grade in English.
2. Settle the privacy matter.
3. Begin as you can, not as you "should."
4. Mundane is also a "way in"—God is in the details.
5. Meditation on an issue often opens the door.
6. Everyday stuff starts you where you are instead of where you aren't.
7. Gratitude often uncorks the fountains of joy.

Organizing Your Spiritual Autobiography

1. Begin at the very beginning—your first glimmers of God.
2. Imagine you are describing a picture album of key moments in your life.

3. Begin with an honest present inventory and trace your roots.
4. Take it by "ages and stages," signposts and captions.
5. Trace the mountaintops *and* the valleys.

Seeking God's Direction

A Prayer Process for Congregational Leaders

"Seeking God's Direction"[1] is a four-week process for congregational leaders who are seeking a vision from God for the future of their congregation. The process involves praying with scripture and discussing how the timeless word of God speaks to what God is calling the congregation to be and do.

A Four-Week Commitment

Leaders covenant to meet for an hour once a week for three weeks, at the time and place most convenient for all. The fourth week they will meet for ninety minutes. They make a covenant, something like the following:

Sample Covenant

- For the next four weeks we will give priority to these meetings and will be present, if at all possible.
- We will honor the time that all are giving by being on time.

---

[1]This prayer process is adapted from a more comprehensive program, "Growing Disciples," created by Judy Turner and Greg Alexander. A manual for "Growing Disciples" is available from Disciples Home Missions, 1-888-346-2631. E-mail: homelandministries@dhm.disciples.org.

• We will honor God by setting aside our agendas and seeking to be totally open and present to God, listening attentively to the scripture.
• We will participate, as God leads us, in sharing thoughts and insights with other members of the group.
• We will take seriously our task to listen for God's leading of our congregation into the future.

Guiding the Weekly Meetings

If the leadership group working with this process is a planning task force, the chair of that task force can guide all four meetings. If the leadership group is the church board, the chair of the board can lead the group. Or, a different member of the group can guide the process each week. The task of the guide is simply to move the group through the process, keeping an eye on the time. The time allotted to each segment in "A Format for Weekly Meetings" is an approximate guideline. Some weeks it may seem right to the guide to spend more or less time on a segment.

A recorder is appointed to bring a notebook, the group journal, each week. At the end of each meeting, the recorder will write in the journal what the group thinks should be recorded. At the end of the fourth week, the leaders will look back through the journal in formulating their direction for the time ahead.

A Format for Weekly Meetings

10 MINUTES   **Discussing** how the group members have seen God at work recently in their lives and in the life of the congregation

25 MINUTES   **Praying** with a scripture passage (concerning the life and mission of the church)

15 MINUTES   **Discussing** the implications of the passage for the group members

5 MINUTES   **Recording** in the group journal

5 MINUTES   **Closing** prayer time, concluding with the Lord's Prayer

More about the Weekly Meetings

DISCUSSING GOD AT WORK

The first 10 minutes help the leaders to focus on God as they think about how they have seen God at work in their own lives and in the life of the congregation recently. It is wise to keep the discussion focused on recent time and avoid lengthy discussions of personal or congregational needs. Stop and pray for the needs, and then move on to more sharing of perceptions of how God is at work.

This discussion builds faith as the evidence mounts that God is at work in some amazing ways. It helps the leaders become more comfortable in talking about spiritual realities. This discussion also helps open minds and hearts to receive the communication of this living, active God as the prayer proceeds.

PRAYING WITH A SCRIPTURE PASSAGE

Leaders enter into a time of praying with scripture based on a form of prayer Christians have used through the ages. This form is called *lectio divina*,[2] which means "divine reading." The steps of the prayer are as follows:

1. **Invoking:** "We come into God's presence, calling on the Holy Spirit to open the eyes and ears of our spirits to receive what God has for us through the Word, so that it becomes God speaking to us here and now."
2. **Reading:** One person reads aloud a chosen passage from the scriptures. All listen, attentive to the Lord now speaking to them.
   SILENCE: Each allows a chosen work or phrase from the reading to repeat itself quietly within.
   SHARING: Each shares the word or phrase, without any elaboration.

---

[2]For more on *lectio divina* see M. Basil Pennington, *Lectio Divina, Renewing the Ancient Practice of Praying the Scriptures* (New York: Crossroad, 1998).

3. **Reading:** Another member of the group reads the same passage.

SILENCE: Each one now reflects for a couple of minutes, asking, "What is the Lord saying to me in this reading with regard to my life today?"

SHARING: Each may share briefly, "I hear the Lord saying…"

4. **Reading:** Another member of the group reads the passage again.

SILENCE: During a few more minutes of silence the group prays, asking, "Lord, what are you saying to us about our mission as a congregation?"

SHARING: Each may share, "I hear the Lord calling us to…"

Recommended Scripture Passages

Week 1: 2 Corinthians 5:16–21
Week 2: Acts 2:38–47
Week 3: Colossians 3:12–17
Week 4: Matthew 25:34–36 and Matthew 28:18–20

DISCUSSING IMPLICATIONS

God has been speaking as the group has prayed, using the scripture passage. What do the messages heard mean for what God is calling the congregation to be and do? Leaders share their insights.

RECORDING IN THE GROUP JOURNAL

What does the group want to record in the group journal about how God has communicated with them during this session? The recorder writes down the input of the group in answer to this question.

The Fourth Week

The fourth week, the group spends an extra thirty minutes after recording their insights in the group journal to work through a process that will culminate in a clearer sense of direction for the congregation.

- The leader asks the recorder to read slowly all the journal entries since the first meeting.
- Everyone reflects in silence for a few minutes on this question: "Do we hear a clear message from God for the future of this congregation?"
- Each may share their response to this question, as the recorder writes the messages on a board so all can see.
- The leader asks, "What are some repeated themes in these messages?"
- The recorder writes the themes on a board so all can see.
- The leader asks, "From these themes, can we write a vision statement that captures what we believe we've heard from God?"
- The recorder writes responses in a notebook.
- A subgroup of two or three leaders is appointed to write the vision statement in finished form to bring to the group the next time the group meets.

The leaders set a date for their next meeting.

The leaders have a time of prayer, praising, and thanking God for how God has been working in their lives in the last month. They ask for God's continuing guidance and empowerment to lead the congregation into the future God desires for them.